50 YEARS
OF
EAST ANGLIAN
OFFSHORE
RACING

A   TRIBUTE
BY
JAN   WISE

Published by Brent Publications 2001
ISBN No: 0 948706 11 2

Printed by Basildon Printing Company Limited
Fleet House, Armstrong Road, Benfleet, Essex SS7 4FH

INTRODUCTION

"Ocean racing has always been one of the toughest - and most expensive sports - that anyone can indulge in. For that reason it has always attracted characteristic, swash-buckling and - sometimes - eccentric individuals".

I am indebted to Ian Dear's recent history of the Royal Ocean Racing Club "The First 75 Years" (Adlard Coles Nautical, 2000) for this stirring and undeniably accurate analysis.

Offshore racing would scarcely be worth remembering, let alone writing about, if it were not for the people who seem to be drawn to this pre-eminently masochistic occupation.

It is a sport which demands a certain attitude and style. From the same source I quote from the work of A.C. 'Sandy' Sandison, a distinguished RORC member (and in his early days a member of the Crouch Yacht Club) who later wrote a book entitled "To Sea in Carpet Slippers".

Sandison's philosophy seems to me to sum up, quite admirably, the ethos of East Anglian racing.It reads:

1) To sail 'Thalassa' (a West Mersea boat) as hard as possible on every occasion.

2) To extract, in the doing of this, the maximum amount of fun and enjoyment.

The East Anglian Offshore Racing Association may not be

as old as the RORC, but over the past 50 years it has performed much the same function for sailors on the East Coast, without the burden of being regarded as a national authority.

When I started to write this account of fifty years of offshore racing on the East Coast several unkind wags enquired whether it would be a history or an obituary.

Sadly, they do have a point. Entries for offshore events have dwindled alarmingly in the last few years, and in 2000 the number of boats racing was not much more than would have turned out during the first few seasons.

At the same time there has been a big swing towards round-the-cans and Olympic style racing.

It is not entirely clear yet whether this is a genuine preference, or simply the inevitable knock-on from the development of new designs and new technology which have put a premium on racing performance at the expense of any cruising friendly role.

It is also a result of the immense social and financial pressures of the late-Twentieth and early Twenty-first Century life-style, to say nothing of the crippling cost of maintaining and manning a conventional top-class racing yacht.

There are other contributory factors, not least the increasing number of women in the sport and the emergence of the 'New Man' who twenty years ago would have swanned off happily without a backward glance to spend a hearty sailing weekend with his mates, but is now expected to take his share of domestic responsibilities and 'quality time' with his young family.

At the time of writing round-the-cans seems temporarily to be in the ascendant. But the spectacle of a whole fleet of full-on offshore racing boats, conjured from the board of the latest fashionable designer, and equipped with all the mandatory bells and whistles for a Transatlantic passage pirouetting demurely around a set of up-river buoys on a Sunday afternoon, always seems faintly risible.

It is certainly not offshore racing, as the East Anglian competitor traditionally understands it.

Although it seems unlikely the huge 80-strong fleets of the Seventies will ever be repeated, there are encouraging signs at the start of the new Millennium of a steadily growing groundswell of support for the traditional style of racing, with a programme of events now more rationally tailored to the needs of competitors.

I hope this continues, and am confident that there will always be those who still relish the tactical and navigational challenge of threading a course through the sandbanks; for whom the magic of making landfall in a foreign port still endures; and for whom the first beer in the North Sea Yacht Club and an exchange of views with other competitors is still reason enough to go to sea.

All that this book purposes is to ensure that some of the more remarkable and colourful characters and achievements of the last 50 years offshore racing on the East Coast are not entirely forgotten.

I am enormously grateful to all those who have given generously of their time to share their memories, and to lend me so much useful materials, in the shape of photographs, handbooks and race instructions, particularly to Sir Peter Blake who at the end of his latest voyage to Antartica has taken the time to write the foreword.

I would also like to apologize to all those with whom I have been unable to make direct contact, and to anyone whose name or reputation I have inadvertently taken in vain.

J.W.

FOREWORD

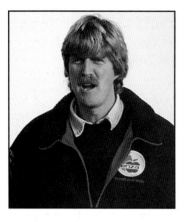

"I came to the UK from New Zealand at the end of the 1960's – a mad-keen young yachtsman wanting to find a job in a yacht design office. I had read all there was to read by Uffa Fox, John Illingworth, Adlard Coles and the like. I had built my own Van de Stadt J.O.G 23 footer, had raced dinghies, one tonners and ocean raced and cruised on yachts owned by family and friends throughout the South Pacific.

Gil Hedges, a great friend of mine in those days in New Zealand and an ex Burnham man, gave me a letter of introduction – and I eventually found myself sailing in Burnham Week on various yachts. An offer of a berth in the Harwich to Ostend followed – my first time in the North Sea at night – with its strong tides, often poor visibility and changeable depths. Having a reliable depth sounder was most important in those days. There was no radar allowed, and GPS hadn't been heard of.

In Ostend I learned of a brand new Hustler 35 – Midas – that was heading for the Solent and then taking part in the Cowes to Cork race. I went on board to meet the skipper – one John Harrison – but found the yacht in a state of disarray – which was explained by one of the crew telling me about a dodgy fish pie they had eaten in the race across.

The trip to the Solent in fog and light winds – having to go right up to the navigation buoys and read off the names to be sure of our position – and then on to win our class to Cork - was a highlight and vital time of my career, and not just because of the win.

I really absorbed the Harrison way of doing things. He was, in many ways, very similar to Gil whom I had grown to admire so much when crewing for him back in New Zealand.

John was a very patient man – never getting upset – never yelling – and a great teacher. Gil gave me a chance and trusted me to be navigator for him on a major ocean race – followed by the Sydney to Hobart.

John was the same and trusted people completely, once he felt they were up to the task.

I was privileged to live with the Harrison family at West Mersea for the next 6 months - spending much of my time racing the inshore waters of East Anglia. It was a very important learning time for me – it helped me hone my skills for what has become a lifetime of racing and cruising in most parts of the world.

Being for such a period with John also helped my appreciation of the man-management aspects that are so important when keeping a crew together and encouraging them – even when the chances of a win are slim.

Did not move into the field of yacht design – I enjoyed my time so immensely with the EAORA fleet and the people involved, that I haven't stopped sailing since.

It set the framework for what has been a great number of very special experiences over many years.

I have just returned from nearly 3 months exploring in the Antarctic – and my eyes are still open wide from the number of new sights I have seen. Later in the year I am heading for the Amazon – because there is still much more to see.

But I know and appreciate how it all began. Many thanks for setting me off on the right path.

I wouldn't have missed it for anything."

Sir Peter Blake

Contents

The Pattinson Cup 1950. The first EAORA race. Left to Right 'Brambling' Donald Spear and Charles Thomas Waldringfield SC, unidentified, 'Hyacinth' David Baddeley RCYC, 'Corrie' Jim Robertson Maylandsea Bay YC, 'Sixpence' Eric Wilde Pin Mill SC, 'Lora' Reverend Groom Waldringfield SC, 'Gwendolen' Arthur Young Pin Mill SC, 'Kestrel' John Howard Pin Mill SC, 'Naushabah' Martin Slater Pin Mill SC, 'Skugga'

viii

CHAPTER ONE

SETTING UP

".....an organisation which would concentrate purely on cruiser racing and offshore events....."

OFFSHORE RACING was in existence on the East Coast long before the arrival of EAORA, but was confined to a few events organised by individual clubs up and down the coast, such as the Crouch Yacht Club's Houghton Cup.

This event, founded in 1911, is claimed to be the oldest established offshore race sailed in British waters, although much depends upon how one defines such an activity, and whether or not it was undertaken by amateur or professional crews.

Another early fixture which long pre-dates EAORA is the Royal Corinthian YC's Thames Estuary Race, inaugurated in 1932.

The last shots of the European War had hardly died away when yachts began to creep out of the dykes and ditches in which they had been laid up during hostilities.

The RORC held its first post-war fixture on the East Coast with the Harwich-Hook Race in 1946.

Many East Anglian owners struggling to rebuild their lives found the RORC programme somewhat too exacting. What they wanted was offshore courses of about 60 miles which could be managed in a normal weekend.

One of the earliest of these was the Pin Mill Sailing Club's Shipwash-Galloper Race, sailed on July 16th 1949. The race attracted 22 yachts in two classes. The start time was 4.00pm and competitors embarking on the 65 mile course were warned that "care should be taken when navigating in the vicinity of the Sunk LV owing to the presence of dangerous wrecks."

One organising body was already in existence. The East Anglian Yacht Clubs Conference met every year to co-ordinate fixtures up and down the coast. These were then passed to the YRA (not yet the RYA) for publication in their annual fixtures list.

Their remit was wide-ranging, embracing more than 20 organisations from Deben Week, and the Brightlingsea and West Mersea Town Regatta Committees, to clubs wishing to hold open dinghy meetings and race weeks. Their area ranged from the Broads to the Crouch, and covered clubs of every size and diversity from tiny up-river Beccles SC and the Waveney and Oulton Broad YC to the prestigious blue-ensign clubs such as the Royal Harwich, and the Royal Corinthian and Royal Burnham on the Crouch.

The idea of an East Anglian Offshore Sailing Association was born at the 1949 Conference meeting when Roger De Quincey, who had taken part in the Shipwash-Galloper event suggested setting up an organisation which would concentrate purely on cruiser racing and offshore events, and offer a series which would attract entries from the whole area.

De Quincey, better known in the sailing world as a successful International 14 sailor and a close friend of the designer Uffa Fox with whom he went to race in the International Sailing

Canoe Series. He owned a small boatyard at Southwold, and was the founder of the short-lived St George Sailing Society.

De Quincey's proposal was enthusiastically supported, and the inaugural meeting was held at the Crown and Anchor Hotel in Ipswich on January 29th 1950.

Fifteen clubs were represented:

The Royal Harwich YC (the most senior club on the East Coast, founded in 1843) was represented by Col. F.L.Tempest, OBE, MC and N.Farrar.

The Royal Norfolk & Suffolk YC (founded in 1859) by Brigadier W.G.Carr, DSO;

St George's SC (founded 1949) by Roger de Quincey;

Aldeburgh YC (founded in 1897) by T.C.Riggs;

Waldringfield SC (founded 1922) by J.S.Alderton, R.Garnham, M. Spear and A.D.(Donald) Spear, who also represented the **Deben YC** (founded 1838).

Felixstowe Ferry YC (founded 1931) were represented by J.C.Rowbotham and F.J.Pearce;

Orwell Yacht Club (founded 1918) by F.R.Chapman and J.Sycamore;

Pin Mill SC by Kingsley Ballard and G.B.(Brian) Humby;

Wivenhoe SC (founded 1921) by J.B. Williams and H.R.Pawsey; From the Blackwater came the **Blackwater SC** represented by H.V. (Viv) Terry, and **West Mersea YC** represented by Geoff Pattinson. Both clubs were founded in 1899.

Walton & Frinton YC (founded 1920) were represented by Mrs E.Davies.

From a little further down the coast, the **Crouch YC** (founded in 1907) was represented by W.D.Baddeley and M.N.Sheard who also spoke on this occasion for the **Royal Burnham YC** (founded 1895).

Others who had indicated interest in the new Association

but were not actually present at the meeting included Robert Bond of the **Norfolk Broads YC**, R.V.Cook of the **Colne YC** and R.C.Frost of **Harwich and Dovercourt SC**.

Amongst many interesting characters at this inaugural meeting was one young man who would play a pivotal part in the whole organisation for the next fifty years, and, in 2001 is still revered as an 'elder statesman' and general benefactor.

Left to Right: 'Skugga', 'Brambling' (D.Spear & C.H.Thomas), 'Nausikar', 'Melody A' (Brig. W.G.Carr), 'Kestrel' (J.Howard).

Mike Spear, then aged 22, who accompanied his father to the meeting was already an experienced sailor and a regular member of the crew of 'Brambling' which would win the new Association's individual championship three times in the early years.

After his father's death in 1959 he became an owner and regular competitor on the circuit with a variety of boats, amongst them 'Maleni' in which he won Class II in 1964. Fifteen years later Mike would become Chairman of the Association, and from 1968

4

as the owner and developer of Suffolk Yacht Harbour at Levington in 1968 Mike has continued to provide unstinting help and support to all East Anglian sailors.

He is a prime example of those who have loyally supported the East Coast through thick and thin and have put back in generous measure as much as they gained from the sport.

Martin Slater, Commodore of Pin Mill SC was elected as chairman of the meeting, and in response to a motion by Roger de Quincey, seconded by T.C. Riggs it was unanimously decided to form an East Anglian Offshore Racing Association.

The stated object was "to co-ordinate and encourage offshore racing by East Anglian clubs, to assist in handicapping, organising and advertising events, and to award points to Clubs upon the results of the seasons' races."

A constitution was drawn up. There were no individual members, but clubs who were interested in offshore racing, or who were already sponsoring races were elected as members, and a committee of representative club members was appointed.

Martin Slater, who was also elected as the Association's first chairman was an immensely experienced offshore yachtsman who 20 years earlier had been a competitor in the first Brightlingsea-Ostend Race, and many others since, including the RORC's North Sea Race in 1946.

Seven others were elected to form the first committee:
The Lowestoft area was represented by Brigadier W.G. Carr of Ditchingham Hall, Norfolk. Southwold was represented by Roger De Quincey; Aldeburgh by T.C. Riggs; the Deben by Donald Spear; Harwich by Brian Humby; the Colne and Blackwater by Geoff Pattinson, and the Burnham area by W.D. (David) Baddeley and M.N. Sheard.

Brian Humby, then living in Waterloo Road, Ipswich also took on the combined post of secretary and treasurer.

Author's Note: Fifty years on I am greatly indebted to him for his memories of competing in the Shipwash-Galloper Race in the veteran gaff-rigged 'Henriette" owned by Dick Greenland as well as for the loan of some of his early photographs of East Anglian racing.

Martin Slater's 'Naushabah'

The annual subscription for each member club was set at 2 guineas.

Confidence in the future of the new Association was boosted when Colonel F.L. Tempest, Commodore of Royal Harwich YC offered to provide a Challenge Cup for the club with the highest number of points in each season.

The delegates also approved a fixture list for the 1950 season. West Mersea YC were responsible for three fixtures. These were the newly established Pattinson Cup presented by Geoff Pattinson for a race from the Crouch to West Mersea and the Buckley Goblets, presented by J.M. Buckley for an end-of-season race to Ostend. Both had been sailed for the first time in 1949, and in addition there was the Club's established Sunk Race.

The programme of "offshore and passage races" was published in a small 15 page handbook, printed by the East

Anglian Daily Times at Ipswich, and priced at one shilling.

The first race of the inaugural season, sailed on May13th 1950 was the Pattinson Cup, a 49-mile course from Burnham to West Mersea via the NE Gunfleet.

It was open to bona fide cruisers over 18ft LWL.

Next, on May 20th came the Royal Corinthian YC's Thames Estuary Race, a 95 mile round trip starting from Burnham at the gentlemanly hour of 13.20.

The course read "Leave Longsand Head Buoy to starboard; Kentish Knock light buoy to starboard; South Knock Buoy to starboard; thence through S. Edinburgh Channel, leaving N.E.Shingles Buoy to port; thence cross into Barrow Deep leaving Knock John Buoy and South Knob Buoy both to starboard. Leave Wreck Buoy to port, thence through Whitaker Channel, leaving Whitaker Bell Buoy to port, thence to finish at Burnham."

The prize for this marathon was "a Laurel Wreath to be held for one year" (which probably explains the design of the subsequent and more permanent trophy). Once again entries were limited to those of not less than 18ft rated LWL .

The third race of the season was a 47-mile race from Harwich to Lowestoft via the Shipwash LV given by the Royal Norfolk & Suffolk Yacht Club, for the East Coast Dragon Challenge Cup.

A week later on Saturday June 17th the RN & SYC also hosted the Smith's Knoll Race, a 52-mile race for the RNSYC's Challenge Cup which offered classes for Cruisers and Dragons.

Next came the Crouch Yacht Club's Houghton Cup, on June 24th. This was by tradition an 82-mile night race starting at 4pm which took the fleet to and from the Crouch on a circuit around the Sunk and Cork Light vessels. The trophy for this race, the oldest, and amongst the toughest of the season was originally given by Sidney Houghton in 1911.

Sidney Houghton was a remarkable character. In 1921 he made a memorable single-handed transatlantic crossing from Halifax, Nova Scotia to Burnham. The trip, which lasted 25 days, was made in his newly acquired 21 ton (TM) cutter 'Neith', designed and built by the legendary Herreshoff in Rhode Island in 1908. In those early days, when there was much less commercial shipping about, the traditional Houghton Cup course around the light vessels was not considered unduly hazardous.

John Booth, still sailing at the age of 80, who has been a member of Royal Burnham YC for 70 years remembers competing in the 21st annual race for the Houghton Cup in 1937.

He recalls one of the competitors being run down by the train ferry out of Harwich, and that crews spent much of the night shining feeble torch lights onto their sails as an aid to visibility.

Since those days the huge growth of marine traffic into Harwich and the Port of Felixstowe has rendered this race (and indeed many others) no longer viable on safety grounds.

Nor is it easy to persuade modern competitors to take part in a night race.

Competition for the Houghton Cup has gone through many re-thinks and revisions without quite finding a settled slot in the annual programme. In recent years it has become a day-race during Burnham Week, a relegation which would without doubt have appalled its original donor.

West Mersea's Sunk Race, starting and finishing at the Nass Beacon but taking in the same circuit of lightships was scheduled for July 8th. The trophy was the Coulton Challenge Cup.

On July 22nd came the Pin Mill Sailing Club's Shipwash-Galloper Race, a 65-mile circuit around the two light-vessels starting and finishing in Harwich, for the Slater Cup. There were two classes, for yachts over and under 25ft rated LWL.

'Naiande'

On August 12th Felixstowe Ferry SC were the hosts for the 50 mile Shipwash-Longsand Head Race, starting off Woodbridge Haven and finishing off Felixstowe Dock.

Still in the same area of operations on August 20th came the Shipwash Trophy Race offered by the St George's Sailing Society. This 50 mile event started off Southwold Harbour, leaving the Aldeburgh Nares buoy and the Shipwash Light-vessel to starboard, and finishing off Lowestoft Harbour.

Not much seems to be known about the St George's Sailing Society, which seems to have been something of a private fiefdom for Roger de Quincey, who lived at Halesworth. He is principally remembered on the East Coast as the designer and builder of 'St George', a Dragon class look-alike which he hoped would catch on as an offshore racer. (For more about St George, see Chapter 2).

Next came the Lowestoft-Aldeburgh Race, hosted by the Aldeburgh SC and the RN & SYC, a 21 mile event held as part of Lowestoft Sea Week.

The race was open to handicap yachts between 4 - 10 tons TM, although larger yachts were also invited to take part if they wished.

The race finished off the South look-out Coastguard Station at Aldeburgh, and the handbook notes that "Pilotage into the river at Shingle Street would be provided at a nominal charge by Aldeburgh YC."

The final race of the season was West Mersea's Buckley Goblets, then as always with a Friday morning start for the 90 mile passage whose only marks were the N E Gunfleet and the Longsand Head buoy. Because of its nature only boats with a RORC rating (i.e. not less than 24ft LWL) were allowed to compete.

In addition to the various trophies, personal medallions, and tankards on offer, several clubs offered money prizes. Of these the RNSYC's Harwich-Lowestoft Race seems to have been the most valuable, with £5 to the winner, £2.10s.0d to second place and £1.10s.0d for third. For their Smith's Knoll Race, in addition to money prizes starting at £4, they offered a silver spoon for each prizewinner.

All the races shown in the programme, with the exception of the Lowestoft-Aldeburgh Race counted as qualifying events for the Royal Harwich's Challenge Cup, which was offered to the member club having the largest number of points during the season, with a maximum of four boats in any four races to count.

In addition there was the Association's Points Prize for the individual yacht with the highest number of points during a season's racing.

Points were awarded on the basis of one for every starter yacht beaten, with a bonus of 5, 3 and 2 points for 1st, 2nd and 3rd places.

Handicapping in these early days was a somewhat hit or miss affair. In theory races were sailed under the YRA system using a Time on Time basis. Time Handicap Correction factors were to be calculated from RORC ratings, or for those without, a YRA rating. But individual clubs seem to have indulged in a happy little habit of adjusting the ratings during the season, and had to be sternly warned that such changes must be submitted to the Association for approval before being applied!

The man charged with sorting out these conundrums was Major Hugh Crane, who was to serve the Association in this capacity for many years.

The last three pages of the inaugural handbook gives a list of speed figures and TCF's for almost a hundred boats, although whether all of these ever actively raced is not known.

So far as safety was concerned there were just three Special Regulations.

Apart from the usual disclaimer that every competing yacht must be seaworthy and fitted and sailed with proper precaution, and asserting the right of the Committee to refuse the entry of any yacht without giving their reasons, it was specified that at least one life-buoy with a self-igniting light must be carried on deck within easy reach of the helmsman for instant use.

Boats were to comply with Board of Trade regulations regarding navigation lights and fog signals, particularly at night, and as it was admitted that these lights might be obscured by headsails owners were enjoined to have "powerful electric torch kept handy to be shown on the sails when necessary." So far as life-lines were concerned, in small yachts where these were not permanently fitted, the booklet noted "a reasonably satisfactory substitute may be obtained by rigging lines from taffrail to main shrouds and a single line from mast to stem head. Any reasonable arrangements will be accepted."

Under the heading 'Equipment' it was specified that a dinghy must be included, and must be of a kind reasonably adequate having regard to the size of the yacht. This dinghy must be fitted with adequate buoyancy, and added "two or more petrol tanks lashed under the thwarts may be used......."

Collapsible dinghies were allowed, if fitted with permanently inflated buoyancy equipment.

Any yachts too small to carry a dinghy on deck were allowed to tow one, and would be eligible for a towing allowance of 5% of MR.

Right from the beginning the social element which has always been such a feature of East Coast racing was in evidence, with notices of pre and post race suppers and dinners being laid on for competing yachts in all the clubs on the circuit.

Only brief details of the first season survive in Martin Slater's Chairman's report to the first annual general meeting.

The first race for the Pattinson Cup attracted 18 starters, but only 6 boats finished, the beat down the Whittaker and Swin being described as "too much for most boats."

Ten of the eleven races were sailed without incident, but Pin Mill SC's Shipwash-Galloper was hit by atrocious weather some five hours after the start and there were numerous retirements along the 17-mile leg from the Shipwash to the Galloper which was a dead plug into a southerly gale.

Martin Slater's report briefly records "A dark and stormy night. 20 starters, 5 finished."

Amongst the handful who completed the race was Donald Spear & Charles Thomas with 'Brambling' which was the only boat in Class II (then 25ft and under rated LWL) to finish, and took the Slater Cup for the fastest corrected time. The race was remarkable for another fine feat of seamanship which seems to epitomise the spirit of East Anglian racing.

The heroes of the hour were the crew of W. le Blanc-Smith's Robb-designed Bermuda sloop 'Matariki'.

When the yacht was almost up to the Galloper light vessel an accident to the rudder stock left her without any means of steering, whereupon, her crew, by sheer perseverance and a great deal of ingenuity, sailed her back home to Pin Mill steering solely by changing sail combinations and sheet trimming.

The account from the Pin Mill SC archives continues "Although they arrived some 48 hours late, and very tired, the satisfaction of having accomplished such a feat amongst the shoals of the Suffolk Coast must be well worth the effort."

The best race of the season seems to have been the WMYC Ostend Race in which Slater noted "Jocasta averaged 9 knots." This was the 54ft yacht newly built in 1950 by Thorneycrofts of Southampton for Geoff Pattinson of West Mersea. The winner from 12 starters was 'Thalassa' (Alan Baker) from 'Brambling'.

Entries for the season averaged 10 yachts per race, with 6.5 finishing. Intriguingly the statistics also record without further explanation "Average number rescued by lifeboats etc 0.3"

At the end of the season The Royal Harwich Points Cup was presented by Commodore Colonel Tempest to West Mersea YC, with 170 points, and was received by past-Commodore Leonard Nalder. The runners up were Waldringfield SC with 98 points.

A Silver Plaque for the best individual performance of the season was presented to Donald Spear and his brother-in-law C.H. (Charles) Thomas with 'Brambling' (51 pts). The runners-up were 'Fireflame' (44 pts) Mystery of Meon (38pts) 'Thalassa (35pts) and 'Sixpence' (33pts).

'Brambling' a 12-ton Gauntlet, built at the Berthon Boat Co. in Lymington in 1935, was to win the championship for her

Vernon Powell

owners twice more, in 1952 and 1955, always in hot competition with Spear's great rival Vernon Powell and 'Naiande' a Mystery class cutter designed by Robert Clark, built by the Sussex Yacht Works in 1938.

The Mystery class was extremely successful, and several more were built including 'Mystery of Meon'.

At the time of writing in 2000 it is good to note that 'Mystery of Meon' has recently been entirely refurbished by John Munns, of Fox's Marina, Ipswich and restored to her original specifications. A sister-ship is nearing completion after a major rebuild in the hands of Jonathan Dyke, harbourmaster at Suffolk Yacht Harbour.

Talking to both Donald's son Mike Spear, and Vernon's son David Powell, one gets the impression that both learned their sailing in the proverbial "School of Hard Knocks".

Going to sea with either of these tough paternal sea-dogs can hardly have been an easy or comfortable option, especially when the younger generation were expected to battle the elements on the foredeck while their skippers were sometimes inclined to prefer a chair in the wheelhouse with a glass of something warming.

"Frankly, it was Hell" David recalled, "To finish was an achievement, to win was a bonus."

All the boats in these early years had been built before the War, and were designed for cruising rather than racing. Wherever possible crews worked regular watches. There was no such thing as worrying about weight distribution or sitting out on the weather decks. Boats were frequently over-canvassed and were thought to sail just as well when heeled than upright. The general 'gung-ho' approach was emphasized by Mike Spear. "Father did not hold with reefing" he recalled.

Mike also recalled that any crew members who had dined not wisely but too well ashore were liable to find themselves lashed in the lee scuppers for the trip home, where repeated washing down with every wave that came aboard was guaranteed to sober up even the worst offender.

At the end of 1950 the Association could congratulate itself on a successful first season.

The only major matter for discussion at the first AGM in November was (then as now) the system of handicapping.

Suggestions were sought for any improvements to the YRA system of measurement and handicapping currently in use, and the Association was asked to do everything it could to encourage clubs to adopt this sytem for regattas as well as for their off-shore races "thus eliminating the hit or miss methods now in force."

"It was desirable", said Chairman Martin Slater, "that all yachts should eventually be measured and rated according to the RORC rules."

The meeting approved a suggestion from Geoff Pattinson of West Mersea for a new race across the North Sea from Harwich to Ostend. Royal Harwich YC agreed to organise the event, and the Association gratefully accepted the offer of a trophy from J.C. (Jack) Rowbotham, a stalwart club supporter (who is remembered with gratitude by Trinity House keepers for his record of having made the annual trip to carry Christmas fare to the crew of the Sunk Lightship for no less than fifty years).

Thus ended the first chapter in the Association's history.

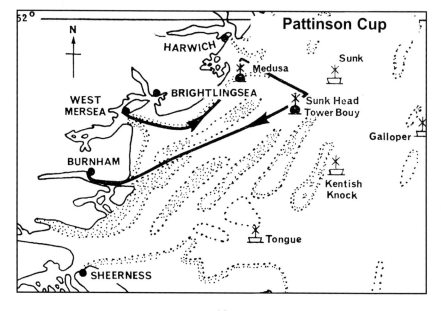

CHAPTER TWO

THE FIRST TEN YEARS

"...We were sodden before we got to the Beach End buoy...."

IT IS difficult at this remove of time to remember the problems and difficulties which faced the sailing community as it struggled to get back to the real world after the Second World War.

Many clubs had been in abeyance during hostilities, or had been kept running on a shoe-string despite all the difficulties and shortages by a handful of elderly local members.

Some Clubhouses, such as the Royal Burnham and the Royal Corinthian on the Crouch were taken over by the Services, a relationship commemorated by the gift of the HMS St Matthew Cup presented for an inter-club team race between the five resident Burnham clubs, which is still contested annually.

At West Mersea where sailing was prohibited from April 1940 until June 1945 the Clubhouse was used as an Officers Mess, while Nisseň huts erected in the gardens were used by the Beach Landing Training Company stationed on the island from 1942.

Other outbuildings and the club launch were also taken

17

over, and it is recorded that by cultivating a part of the Club's garden, and other land in Firs Chase, the Club Steward and a part-time gardener managed between them to grow sufficient vegetables to meet the needs of members and their guests.

Few people now remember the shortages of every type of consumer goods, and the strangling reels of red tape which made it impossible to obtain materials to refurbish club buildings, or to refit neglected boats which had been laid up for the duration, or commandeered for Service use. It was difficult even to obtain a permit to buy fuel.

A sidelight is thrown on the period by Michael Emmett, a Maldon fisherman who wrote in "Blackwater Men" of his father's experiences in 1946, when after being discharged from the Royal Navy he attempted to start a yacht chartering business on the Blackwater, using his traditional gaff-rigged ketch 'Topsy'.

The 52ft 'Topsy' had escaped being commandeered during the war, largely because when laid up in 1939 she had been put into her berth on such a high Spring tide that it was almost impossible to get her out again.

This cunning ploy also saved her from the fate which befell many yachts which were immobilised by having a plank or two removed. In these early post-war years when the seas were still mined and there was no such thing as a regular cross-Channel ferry service, most of Arthur Emmett's passengers were simply looking for any way to reach the Continent after having been confined to the British islands for so long.

The chartering business was way ahead of its time, and did not last long, but Arthur's memories of this period abound with descriptions of creeks and harbours still filled with wrecks and the other detritus of war, and to the constant need to be alert for floating mines. Even several years after the end of the War it was still necessary to restrict navigation to the swept channels.

When hostilities ended West Mersea YC was one of the first clubs on the East Coast to start racing again, although at first this was restricted to day-boats because of the risk of mines.

In August 1945 the Admiralty announced that sailing and rowing in craft of up to 2 tons would be permitted on the Crouch and Roach.

Cruiser racing took a little longer to get going.

The first RORC post-war North Sea Race was held in 1946. Several West Mersea boats took part including 'Thalassa', 'Brambling', and 'Mindy'.

Replacing the prewar Maas Race, the course finished at the Hook of Holland, and it is recalled that the Sailing Instructions had to be referred for approval to the Admiralty's Minesweeping Division, who recommended that steel-hulled yachts should be banned, in case they attracted the attentions of magnetic mines!

Nothing daunted, the race proved extremely popular and attracted seven entries in the large class and twelve in the smaller class.

Mike Spear who took part remembers having to consult a big book issued by the Admiralty which listed all the swept channels.

"We had to stick rigidly to the channels. In the 1946 race we went right up to the Smith's Knoll lightvessel, and then south again to the Galloper before crossing to the Hook - it was up one way, and down the other, you couldn't just go where you wanted to."

Even when most of the minefields had been swept there was still the potential danger of running across a mine which had broken adrift, a threat not entirely absent fifty years on, when most summer seasons see the occasional mine disturbed from the sea-bed and caught in fishing nets, requiring a call-out to the Army Bomb Disposal Squad.

Sailing was tough, and offshore racing was not for wimps. Just as modern climbers are fascinated and appalled by the photographs of Victorian mountaineers, who apparently conquered their peaks dressed in little more than a stout tweed suit, modern sailors encased in their top-of-the-range breathable, flexible ocean outfits, complete with all the necessary bells and whistles, would scarcely believe how minimal was the protective clothing on offer in the immediate post-War years.

The only waterproof clothing was the rigid long black oilskin frocks worn by fishermen over their leggings and thigh-length waders.

Mike Spear vividly remembers the bitter cold on that first Hook race, when they faced a 5-6 north-easterly on the nose all the way to Smith's Knoll.

"We were sodden, before we got to the Beach End buoy" he recalls.

Later, when ex-Army surplus stores began to open up, sailors were grateful for the lightweight waterproof anti-gas capes which could be picked up cheaply, although they were far from ideal not least on account of the way in which the bulge on the back designed to accommodate an Army pack flapped in the wind.

In the Fifties "submarine suits" became available. "They were good, although they were a bit heavy and cumbersome" Mike remembered.

Adequate wet-weather gear was not the only problem.

Yachts were still expected to carry a tender. There was an additional time allowance if you could not get this aboard and had to tow it. Collapsible or inflatable dinghies were far into the future.

Dinghies were usually designed specifically to fit over the coachroof, which did little for their rowing capabilities, and it is hard to imagine that they would realistically ever have been much help in saving the crew in a crisis.

'Brambling' carried a 7ft pram, hardly the most practical craft for laying out an anchor when required.

Most yachts at this date were rigged as cutters, mainly because it made sails easier to handle, when cotton sail-cloth could soak up three times its own weight in water.

Recalling arrangements aboard his father's yacht 'Naiande' David Powell said "The cutter rig was preferred. We only had tiny bottom-handle winches, and they were simply not man enough for the job. The sheets were wire, with rope tails, and you had to get the wire onto the drum".

Unusually for her time 'Naiande' carried a masthead jib, with a huge overlap, which gave her a fine performance but was very difficult to handle.

New materials began to come in towards the end of the decade, but they did not always live up to their promise, and mistakes were made in handling them.

Mike Spear remembers the glee aboard 'Brambling' (whose only concession to modern materials was a nylon spinnaker) when the new mainsail made by Ken Gowan for 'Naiande' fell to bits very shortly after its first outing.

The sail had been cut from a roll of experimental Terylene cloth developed for use aboard 'Sceptre' the British 1958 Admiral's Cup contender, but the panels had been stitched with cotton thread which was soon cut to bits by the new wonder-cloth.

Despite all the problems and shortages, the Corinthian spirit prevailed, and standards were maintained whenever possible.

At the end of a race, no matter how late one arrived, how wet or rough the trip had been, or how difficult it was to get ashore, it was a matter of pride amongst competitors to dig out their formal yachting dress on arrival and to make a smart entrance for dinner and prizegiving at the host club.

As Mike Spear remembers "Offshore was offshore then. Most people left home early on Friday evening and sailed their boats to wherever the next morning's race was due to start. We would often have just a couple of hours sleep at Shore Ends before the start, which might be anything between 6.30am - 9.30am to catch the tide".

Fifty years on how things have changed!

John Harrison of West Mersea put his finger on one of the reasons when he told me "It was a hang-over from the War. We had all been on active service, and were looking for a new challenge. We didn't want to settle down, and we craved adventure. And don't forget that people had been trapped at home for years, and couldn't go where they wanted. The freedom to just B.........off and go wherever you wanted was something special. People don't need that now, so why go out to get wet and cold?"

John, who gave the author immense help, but sadly died whilst this book was in preparation, started his sailing career with the Dabchicks SC when his family had a holiday home on Mersea Island. He was keen on racing and built his own dinghy.

Later he joined West Mersea YC, and crewed with Vernon Powell in 1952 before he purchased his first yacht.

This was a 35 footer Scandinavian type metre design 'Troll' built in Denmark in 1907. Just before he died in October 2000 John was delighted to discover that the beloved little boat was still around, and undergoing a total refit in Burnham in the ownership of David Crossland, an enthusiastic supporter of traditional sail.

No-one could have been more closely associated with EAORA over its first half-century than John. His memory and power of almost total recall of every race and every craft in which he had competed was truly phenomenal, and I am greatly indebted to him for many of the stories and incidents in this book.

He was an excellent journalist, contributing regularly to the yachting press. His tally of 8 Fastnet Races, and 30 North Sea Races must surely be a record.

Over the years he successfully campaigned boats for many owners, as well as on his own behalf, notably with 'Gunsmoke' in which he won Class II in 1968, and 'Ricochet' in which he won the EAORA season's championship in 1971.

In a career which has spanned every aspect of the yachting industry from the smallest little boat to highly successful blue-water cruising yachts equipped with every state-of-the-art navigational aid, John always retained his enthusiasm for working the channels and swatchways of the East Coast.

Looking back with some nostalgia to the rudimentary equipment of the early days he told me "In a small boat the effect of the tide was absolutely crucial. You could make big gains if you used the senses God gave you to look at the water and see what was happening, and whether or not the flood had started."

Pilotage was a hit or miss affair, especially across the North Sea to Ostend.

"You could fetch up two or three miles either side, desperately trying to work out which way the entrance was" he recalls. "Some navigational methods owed more to luck than judgement, especially in the case of the skipper who is alleged to have sailed on in fog until he could hear the waves breaking on the beach, and hailed a passing horseman for directions to the Ostend pierheads".

On another occasion, when 'Corrie' had unexpectedly got ahead of John's boat in the final stages he recalls skipper Jim Robertson declaring that his lucky break was due to having recognised the smell of the fish-factory on the coast near Nieuport!

With minor amendments here and there the first season had set the pattern for the next few years.

The 1951 programme was enlarged to include 14 events, such as a 24 hour race organised by the Crouch YC for their Stanley Kiver Cup, for which yachts might start from Burnham, Leigh-on-Sea, West Mersea or Harwich. This novel idea did not count as a qualifier for the season, and does not seem to have been repeated.

No doubt some of the regular East Anglian competitors also took part in the 1951 RORC Harwich-Hook Race which has a special place in the history of the Royal Harwich YC.

Fortuitously the race was scheduled for the day on which the King and Queen of Denmark were due to leave Parkeston Quay after a State Visit to Britain.

A naval guardship 'HMS Bleasdale' was in attendance. Ships in the harbour were dressed overall, and Landguard Fort fired a salute as the Royal yacht 'Kronpriz Frederik' sailed away escorted by HM Ships 'Opportune', 'Zephyr' and 'Savage'.

Those were the days!!

Once again it proved a good season; only one race was cancelled owing to bad weather, and the new Harwich-Ostend fixture proved especially popular, being won by Eric Wilde of Pin Mill SC with 'Sixpence'.

Total entries were slightly up on the first year, and West Mersea YC were once again the winners of the RHYC Points Cup.

The individual championship went to Vernon Powell in 'Naiande' which he purchased in 1950 from Bernard Hayman the yachting writer and long-serving editor of 'Yachting World'.

'Naiande's' first race was the Pattinson Cup of 1951 which she won. Vernon's 14 year old son David was among the crew.

David's earliest sailing was done on the Norfolk Broads, but like so many others he was prevented from working his way up through the dinghy racing scene by the Second World War.

"I was always mad keen, and I was lucky to be able to start

so young, but the War stopped everything in its tracks" he said "We would all have been much better sailors if we had started in dinghies."

Nevertheless the early years included crewing a Hornet dinghy in the first National Championships, held at the Royal Corinthian YC in Burnham, when they succeeded in taking two races off the previously unbeaten (and widely regarded as unbeatable) Beecher Moore.

"It was very creditable that offshore racing got going again so quickly after the War" he said "It was desperately difficult. All the boats had been laid up, and many were in very poor condition".

Navigation was a major problem, and more races were lost on this score than by poor sailing.

"It was extremely difficult to get it right. If you actually found Belgium you felt like Christopher Columbus" he remembers. The only instruments at the time were a primitive radio fitted with a BEME loop aerial on which it was occasionally possible to pick up signals from the radio beacons fitted to the light-ships.

Races to Ostend finished between the two pier-heads, and yachts were expected to take their own time. David recalls that bomb damage was still visible in the town; there were no pontoons in the harbour, and the North Sea YC occupied a small wooden shed.

David's subsequent offshore career appears in a later chapter, but his account of his first Fastnet Race at the age of 17 aboard the veteran East Coast entry 'Thalassa' with Alan Baker, then Commodore of West Mersea, gives a wonderful flavour of the offshore racing world at that time.

'Thalassa's' Fastnet form went back to 1927, and she was certainly not expected to take any prizes in a fleet which by this time was beginning to include the first post-war high flyers.

But her veteran crew were just as determined as anyone else to put up a good show. 'The Thalassians' as they called themselves, were a formidable bunch.

On this occasion the crew included Iorys Hughes, an architectural and structural engineer, who was closely associated with the design of the Mulberry Harbours which played such a vital role in the success of the D-Day landings in Normandy.

Other projects in which he was involved included Wembley Stadium, the Hyde Park Underpass, and the Dock in which the 'Cutty Sark' now resides in Greenwich.

Hughes, a notable early member of the RORC, retired to West Mersea in 1966 and died in 1977. He is commemorated at Deganwy, in North Wales from where he originally came, and also at the Museum of the Normandy Invasion at Arromanches.

Another remarkable character aboard was A.C.'Sandy' Sandison, remembered as a valued crewman aboard such RORC immortals as 'Bloodhound', 'Foxhound', and 'Fandango' whose talents as a cook and raconteur were greatly in demand. He worked in the Bank of England and was the author of a book of wonderful reminiscences about offshore racing entitled "To Sea in Carpet Slippers" (Adlard Coles, 1966).

I have quoted Sandison's philosphy of racing in the Introduction to this book, which bears repeating here, as:

a) Race 'Thalassa' as hard as possible on every occasion, and

b) Extract in the doing of this, the maximum amount of fun and enjoyment.

It is a philosophy which admirably sums up much of what EAORA has always been about.

David recalls that the crew included Buster De Guingand, later a flag officer of the RORC, Sir Jocelyn Bodilly, and John Whalley, whose first wife was the film star Veronica Papworth.

It must have been a baptism of fire for a 17 year old boy.

"They had all done Fastnets before the War. It was very character-forming" was David's dry comment.

It is good to know that at the time of writing 'Thalassa' is still going strong, and is now in Ireland in the ownership of Alan Baker's son-in-law.

At the second AGM a few anomalies were ironed out, but basically things went on as before.

Most importantly rules were laid down for an Inter-Club Championship, which was to be decided on the points scored by a maximum of three yachts from each club in any four races.

More contentiously, delegates voted by a narrow margin to set a limit of five races from which yachts could count points towards the individual championship.

Colonel Sidney Marks of the Blackwater SC kindly offered a new Challenge Cup for the best performance during the season, leaving it to the committee to judge on what basis this should be judged.

The trophy eventually became the much coveted Blackwater Trophy for the overall individual championship, won by more than 30 different owners over the next 50 years.

Two further decisions from this meeting throw an interesting light on the way in which racing was starting to develop.

The first was to ask J.C. Buckley, the donor of West Mersea's coveted Buckley Goblets to allow the minimum LWL to be reduced from 24ft to 18ft so that smaller yachts were not debarred from the points competition.

The second was to follow the example of Pin Mill's Shipwash-Galloper Race by bringing in a separate class for gaff-rigged yachts for every race... "in view of the unsuitability of these yachts to compete with modern types......"

The 1953 season was also, of course, Coronation Year.

Despite the Royal event which was felt to have affected entries in the earlier races, the committee could congratulate themselves that the number of yachts taking part in the points competition, and the average number of starters per race, had both shown an increase.

West Mersea continued to dominate the club championship, with Maylandsea Bay YC as runners-up. Vernon Powell and 'Naiande' were again successful in the individual championship.

The first winner of the new trophy for boats under 23ft LWL was 'Watertrekker' owned by Polish-born Resistance fighter and refugee Jerzey 'George' Polturak of Royal Burnham.

George was a great character, who started sailing as a child on the Black Sea, and also sailed extensively with Maurice Laing, despite the handicap of an artificial leg.

His daughter Francesca, now living in Australia, recalls "Dad bought 'Watertrekker' in 1952, I think. She was built in Holland in 1947 of teak. Originally she had a gunter rig, but although she raced quite successfully Dad wanted a more efficient windward performance, so he got Alan Buchanan to design a copy of a Dragon rig for the boat. And the rest, as they say, is history."

Francesca recalls learning to row at the age of six, in Ostend harbour, in 'Watertrekker's' little green collapsible dinghy, having travelled over on the ferry with her mother Viva, when that long-suffering lady could no longer be persuaded to crew for her father in a "24ft sieve which went through rather than over the water, and took twice as long as any other boat to arrive, and which created in her a lifelong detestation of the sport!"

The runner-up for this new trophy was Jim Robertson of Braintree, owner of the infamous Clyde 30 'Corrie' whose exploits remain legendary to this day.

Built in 1908 to a design by William Fife, 'Corrie' always

'Watertrekker' - George Polturak

wintered in a mud-berth in the Ballast Hole at Heybridge, where irrespective of the owner's own frequent absences, attributable to the need to play his home-made double bass in an amateur dance band to raise the money needed to keep the boat going, his hapless crew were expected to have her ready for the RORC's North Sea Race at Whitsun.

I am indebted to Maurice Perry, archivist and longest-standing member of the Blackwater SC who vividly recalls sitting around a glowing Tortoise stove in the clubhouse on winter Saturday evenings, busy with the rest of the crew splicing, varnishing blocks and mending sails.

In looks much like a cross between a Dragon and a J class, 'Corrie' had flush decks, no coach-roof, no engine, and no lifelines. She indulged in a draft of some 7ft, with long overhangs fore and aft.

Maurice describes her as "The wettest ship that ever left the protection of the Ballast Hole."

He recalls:

"Jim could smell his way across the North Sea. He knew by the colour of the ocean just where we were, and if he did chance to be a little doubtful, 'Corrie' knew her own way anyhow.

'Corrie's crew were not wealthy yachtsmen.... however when being entertained in Rotterdam by the Royal Maas YC after the usual North Sea Race weather, Force 8 or 9, we did all sport dinner jackets, as was proper for such an event.

Unfortunately Jim had used his jacket not only for many Saturday evening dance stands, and impregnated it with the essence of various refreshments, but it had also survived a good number of fitting out jobs from time to time."

"Still, Jim was the skipper, and if he was to be well dressed for the occasion the crew had naturally to keep their end up. I remember one wet and cold race, our dinner jackets were stowed in the forepeak which should have been a good place - unfortunately 'Corrie' did leak a bit up the for'ard end, but it is strange just how quickly good quality Moss Bros gear can grow a green mould and lose that expensive look."

"Jim was a good chap, but he did have quirks. Weight was one of his pet subjects. Weight had to be kept out of 'Corrie' by order....hence no engine, but this was somewhat nullified by the inclusion of the biggest double-action pump you ever saw under the cockpit floor. And she needed it!"

Another character who was a 'regular' member of the 'Corrie' crew in the early days was the designer Don Pye of West Mersea, who with his business partner Kim Holman was to be involved in so many innovative new designs in the next two decades. It is good to know that in 1999 'Corrie' was based on the Solent and still going strong. She was still in the Robertson family, having been completely rebuilt by Jim's son James.

David Geaves of Royal Burnham, who began his sailing career in 'Corrie' in 1950 comments "I don't think people nowadays realise how wet boats were then. They were built of wood, and they weren't really built for racing. They worked all the time. You had to have someone on the pumps all the time. I don't

'Corrie'

mean just every 4 hours or so, but continuously throughout your watch." Although 'Corrie's offshore performance was much improved after a winter of modifications in Heybridge Basin which included moving the mast several feet further aft, and shortening the boom, she failed to conform to any modern safety rules. Amongst other eccentricities Jim Robertson is remembered as the inventor of the 'Penguin' hat - a hood constructed from black tarred canvas with a peak made from an aliminium saucepan lid. A proposed modification involved spray deflectors to be fitted to the peak.

Nevertheless David remembers Jim Robertson as one of the toughest and best seamen he had ever encountered, and it is a tribute to his indomitable spirit that so many modern sailors have told me of his exploits.

Although she never seemed to have accrued the same notoriety there was a sister-ship to 'Corrie' in the EAORA fleet. This was 'Mikado' owned by John Gozzett of West Mersea, who has been a supporter ever since with a long line of successful boats, and is now succeeded by his son Robin with 'Destiny of Mersea'. The 1954 season was notable for bad weather, and no races were sailed north of Harwich, but despite this, entries were still creeping up. Post-war boats were beginning to come on the scene, and there was a notable increase in the number of smaller boats.

Indeed it was recorded that these "had carried off all the prizes." This was no doubt a dig as J.W. Noel Jordan's new Swedish designed 25ft sloop 'Martha McGilda' (built by Chippendale Boats at Warsash in 1953) in which he won not only the individual season's championship but also the Barnard Cup.

David Powell remembers that amongst 'Martha McGilda's' crew was the young yachting journalist Bob Fisher of Brightlingsea.

In 1954 West Mersea's hold on the inter-club cup was broken, with the trophy going to the Royal Corinthian. It should be noted in this context that West Mersea boats were very busy elsewhere, winning the prestigious Martin Illingworth Trophy, the RORC's inter-club points trophy for the first time.

The individual runner-up was another new boat, designer Alan Buchanan's 31ft sloop 'Taeping'.

Built in 1954 at R.J. Prior & Son's in Burnham, she set the scene for a long line of distinguished wooden yachts which would come from that yard over the next two decades.

The newcomers were to dominate East Anglian racing for the next few seasons, with 'Martha McGilda' taking both trophies for the second time in 1956, while 'Taeping' won the Barnard Cup in 1955 and 1957 in which year she was also overall champion.

A major event of the 1955 season was the first race for the Amazon Cup, a new team trophy presented by Royal Harwich for a return race from Ostend following the RORC's North Sea Race, sailed over the August Bank Holiday (then celebrated over the first weekend of the month, not as now, the last).

This was not a new trophy, but rather a race to mark the centenary of the first Amazon Cup Race, sailed in 1855. The fabulous piece of silverware was donated by one Andrew Arcedeckne for the Harwich Regatta of that year.

It is strange to think that the Crimean War was still in progress when the 42 ton cutter 'Amazon' sailed a 40 mile course off Harwich in three and three-quarter hours to win the cup for the first time. Further successes also made her the champion yacht for 1855. After this, the trophy disappeared from view for the next 100 years. Fortuitously it re-appeared in the salerooms in the early Fifties, just in time for the Club to buy it back for the double race from Harwich to Ostend and Ostend to Lowestoft to mark its centenary in 1955.

The winners were Donald Spear and his brother-in-law Charles Thomas (always known as 'The Admiral') with 'Brambling'.

Mike Spear remembers the party at his home to celebrate the victory, and his father's horrified re-action when he found the fabulous Cup being used as a punch-bowl!

In later years the Amazon Cup became an inter-club team trophy for the Royal Harwich's annual EAORA race from Harwich to Ostend.

At the 1954 AGM the North Sea Yacht Club were unanimously elected as honorary members of the Association in recognition of the hospitality so freely offered to competitors.

This happy relationship was also celebrated in 1994 to mark the 40th anniversary of the club's election.

At the end of 1955 Donald Spear came to the end of his three years as chairman. He was replaced by Alan Baker.

H.C. Thomas the secretary also resigned, and Alan Buchanan was reluctantly pressed into service.

One feature of the Association's early years which later slipped into abeyance was the annual rally.

This was held in late September, at the end of the racing season and was intended purely as a social event and a chance to get together to float new ideas. A note in the minutes in 1951 makes it clear that the event was intended "for all offshore racing yachtsmen, and was not restricted to those who could actually sail to the rendezvous."

The first of these annual jollies was held at Pin Mill in 1952, and was followed by all the clubs in succession until around 1960 when it was held at the Royal Corinthian. After this it seems to have dropped from the records, probably when the annual general meeting was combined with a dinner and prizegiving.

The 1956 season was notable for bad weather. One race

from Aldeburgh was cancelled for lack of entries, and only two boats turned out for the Thames Estuary Race.

At the AGM it was decided that the time had come to re-allocate some of the trophies, and it was agreed to adopt a class system, with entries divided into three groups by rating.

The class limits were set at 19ft or less than 24ft LWL for Class III, 19-25ft rating, minimum 24ft LWL for Class II, and over 25ft RORC rating for Class I.

Felixstowe Ferry's Barnard Cup was allocated to Class II, where it has remained ever since.

Mr L.T. Daniels offered to present the Carmen Cup for boats of 19ft and under, and it was agreed that a new cup should be procured for Class I. (In the event the Carmen cup was eventually allocated to Class I, and the Gunfleet Trophy was obtained for Class III).

It was further agreed that engraved bronze plaques should be given to the first four boats overall. These 2 inch diameter discs became amongst the most highly prized offerings, often being proudly tackled to a cross-beam on board.

Another icon which emerged from this 1956 meeting was the now well-known 'lightship' logo. The idea came from Alan Buchanan who asked Archie White, an artist and prominent member of West Mersea (and designer of the club's distinctive defaced Red Ensign) to come up with some ideas. The lightship was felt to be a happy choice reflecting the Association's close encounters with most of the lightships in the North Sea.

By 1957 when the annual meeting unanimously elected the Medway YC (founded in 1880); the Royal Engineer YC; and the RNSA based at HMS Ganges at Shotley, the Association could boast 14 member clubs.

It may seem curious to find a Service club listed amongst the 20 or so most senior clubs in the UK. Lloyd's Register of

Shipping names only 21 clubs dating from earlier than 1846, when the REYC (originally the Engineer Boat Club) was founded at Chatham.

In the years after the Second World War the club was a great supporter of offshore sailing, and had a proud record in RORC events, with a succession of Robert Clark designed yachts such as 'Right Royal' (1951) 'Annasona' (1955) and 'Ilex' (1963).

Indeed until recently (and including the notorious 1979 race) club boats had competed in every Fastnet Race since it was first run in 1926.

The Club provided numerous committee and flag officers for the RORC including Brigadier 'David' Fayle who served on the technical sub-committee during the development of the new RORC Rating Rule, and in 1957 became their permanent Rating Secretary with responsibility for all measurement and rating matters.

Another distinguished 'Old Boy' was Colonel Ken Wylie, who raced a succession of boats under the REYC flag, and served as rear commodore 1957-8 and vice-commodore 1961-3.

During the Second World War he was a prisoner of war, and it is recalled that he kept himself sane during his imprisonment in Colditz by designing the yachts he hoped to build after the War.

His tally of 14 Fastnets, a Transatlantic crossing and 50 years of the RORC North Sea Race is probably unequalled.

More than this. On leaving the Army this redoubtable but always intensely modest man became honorary secretary of West Mersea YC where his own contribution, and that of the whole Wylie family, to offshore sailing cannot be underestimated.

His eldest daughter Fiona has accumulated her own distinguished tally of offshore races, and has given many years of service to the sport as a flag officer and ambassador for the RORC.

Vicky, with her husband Tom Jackson, are an offshore

The Wylie family, crew for the 1975 Fastnet

racing legend with their classic veteran 'Sunstone' of which we shall hear more in a later chapter.

To mark the Royal Ocean Racing Club's fiftieth anniversary in 1975 the Wylie family created something of a record with their 'Family Crew' which included Ken Wylie, his three daughters; Fiona, Vicky and Annabel, together with John Wylie, and Vicky's husband Tom Jackson.

The Association is also indebted to the REYC for the long and distinguished services of Brigadier Basil Chichester-Cooke,

'St George'

both on the committee, and later as their honorary auditor into the mid-Eighties.

It was due to Basil's influence that the Association was enabled to hold its annual dinner on several occasions in the magnificent dining-room of the Royal Engineers Mess at Brompton Barracks in Chatham, a setting enriched by the displays at intervals of a few feet on every polished table of the RE's historic silverware, representing battle honours in practically every

sphere of Empire. In addition, Basil was the donor of the Jane's Cup, one of the Association's most prestigious trophies, given in memory of his young daughter "who loved boats." For many years the Jane's Cup was considered so special that it was not presented after the race from Burnham to the Medway, but was held back for special presentation at the annual dinner.

Cannon ball Trophy

It is believed that Jane Chichester-Cooke was the person responsible for finding the cannon ball discovered in the mud of the Medway near Upnor Castle in 1962, which was later identified by the National Maritime Museum as having been fired by a Seventeenth century Dutch warship.

Basil arranged for the cannon ball to be mounted on a plinth of yew, cut from a tree in the grounds of Upnor Castle.

The plinth carries the inscription: "De Ruyter's Cannon

Ball. A ship of De Ruyter's fleet fired this ball against the British fleet in 1667. Recovered near Upnor Castle, Chatham it was returned to Holland in 1962 for annual competition between Dutch and British RORC rated yachts. Presented to the Royal Netherlands YC by a group of Medway yachtsmen of the REYC, RNSA and MYC."

The Cannon Ball Trophy was sailed for by a team of nominated Dutch and British yachts sailing in the Flevo Races in the Ijsselmeer, of which we shall read more in a later chapter.

By the end of 1958 the Association was on a roll; numbers were rising rapidly with an increase of 22 boats, making a total of 66 for the season. West Mersea took the club championship for the second year.

The overall champion was J. Maurice Laing's (later Sir Maurice Laing) famous 37ft sloop 'Vashti' who captured the Barnard Club for three successive years from 1958-60.

Built at Prior's yard in Burnham 'Vashti' went on to win honours and renown on the South Coast (where her distinctive livery earned her the nickname 'the Yellow Peril').

Almost 50 years later she is still around, and looking as elegant as ever as she makes the occasional appearance on the East Coast in races for classic yachts. In 1998 she was awarded the trophy for the Concourse d'Elegance at the Royal Burnham's Whitsun Regatta.

While 'Vashti' dominated Class II, another outstanding yacht, Norman Davis's 'Mindy' took Class I and the Carmen Cup. Built by W. King & Sons in Burnham in 1938 'Mindy' was already twenty years old.

The following year she was featured in the 1959 Yachting World Annual amongst a collection of designs described as vintage and which "on account of their design and performance have become seamarks in the evolution of the ocean racing yacht."

'Mindy' drew her distinction from three sources. Firstly, her racing record; secondly the character of her design; and the fact that she was the creation of F.B.R. (Buster) Brown, a most distinguished amateur architect who owned her from 1939-1953.

During this period she won 29 prizes in 36 starts in RORC and passage races, taking the Ortac Cup for the greatest number of points in the season in 1939, 1948 and 1950.

Another of Buster Brown's designs was 'Galloper' which raced at various times under the ownership of Les Hills and David Powell.

The 1958 season was also remarkable for the emergence of Lieut. John Lawson, RN, a notable competitor who burst onto the scene with his little 'Amoret' to become the first winner of the new Gunfleet Cup for Class III. Posted to the staff of HMS Ganges, the Navy's training establishment at Shotley Point, he was a fine sailor.

He also skippered 'Sea Feather' for HMS Ganges, enabling that shore establishment to win the inter-club competition in 1959, a feat which must have represented many hours and miles of recreational sea-miles allowed to Service personnel, an unimaginable luxury in the straightened world of the Navy of the late 1990's.

'Sea Feather' like the most famous 'Bloodhound' and HMS Collingwood's 'Wal' (later 'Merlin') who both raced extensively on the South Coast at the same period, was one of the 50 Squares - 50 sq.metre racing yachts built at Keil in Germany in 1938 to boost Hilter's yachting ambitions. When hostilities ended these boats were taken over as reparations or spoils of war, and allocated to various Service establishments.

'Sea Feather' was owned nominally by the C-in-C, Nore Command a great supporter of offshore racing who in 1961 would present the Association with the Nore Command Cup for competition on his patch.

There is another story, entirely irrelevant to the East Coast, which the author always cherishes in connection with these 50 Squares, relating to 'Wal' which was skippered by Lt. Cdr. Edmund Spalding. Spalding, a man who always had an eye to the pennies managed to get his charge nominated as the official 'HMS Collingwood' - a move which enabled him both to fly the White Ensign, and to have his yacht maintained "on the books."

Unfortunately this move rather worked against him, when after a couple of seasons of parading his White Ensign around the Solent, thereby forcing large numbers of ships and Very Senior Officers to dip their ensigns in reply as he passed, 'HMS Collingwood' was demoted, and obliged to become 'Wal' whose bills had to be met out of funds for 'Rest and Recreation'.

Although John Lawson only sailed on the East Coast for a couple of seasons while serving at HMS Ganges he left an unforgettable legacy in the shape of the magnificent silver lightship, modelled on the Galloper, which is one of West Mersea's most treasured possessions.

The Lightship.

The light-ship was commissioned from the ship-building firm of Camper & Nicholson who still retained a model-maker. Ironically although he saw the work in progress, owing to the exigencies of a Naval career it was not until 1986 that John Lawson actually set eyes on the finished article.

John and Anne who now live at Newton Ferrers in Devon recalled their time on the EAORA scene in a recent article in West Mersea YC's 'Moliette' which is reprinted below:

"I was serving in HMS Ganges at Shotley in 1958 and raced a little Illingworth & Primrose cutter, all of 19ft 6ins on the waterline. The intrusion into the local racing scene by a boat designed on the South Coast was viewed with a jaundiced eye in some quarters, especially when we won a few races, and the EAORA Class III championship that year.

We didn't even have an outboard motor for much of this first year, and cruised across to Holland with two of us, through the canal from Flushing to Veere and out at the Roompot when there was an entrance there. A bucket on a lanyard was very useful when approaching bridges reluctant to open. Later, in the summer leave, we got as far West as Dartmouth and did a couple of JOG races with a marked lack of success.

1959 started with a single-handed trip to Ostend and back. A home-designed and made vane gear could have worked better, and I remember arriving home very tired .

After that we took racing more seriously with some effect and won the overall EAORA Points Trophy. 'Sea Feather' an elderly Naval 50 Square Metre was also raced with success and between us we won the Club Points for the first, and I believe the only time, for HMS Ganges.

In 'Amoret' we raced with three, one of whom was a Junior Seaman under training, who was really included to keep up appearances and to encourage the Navy to give us all the time off to race. Some enjoyed it, but others couldn't get back ashore quick enough after a race offshore.

The only instruments we had in those days were a dinghy compass (unlit) a B & G echo sounder and D.F. radio. The latter was of limited value except for the beacons on the Hinder lightships which helped to find Ostend. We only drew four feet, so it was over the stern and push if you misjudged the width of the Crouch, or the

'Samuel Pepys'

Mersea Quarters - another good reason for taking a Junior Seaman...."

Remembering 'Amoret' and her dashing young Naval skipper John Harrison recalled one Houghton Cup Race, when he was sailing with Alex and Neil Bailey on the RNSA 24 'Tasman'.

"There was a big south-wester, the tail end of a front coming through, as we set off down the Crouch with a boomed out

44

jib. 'Amoret' kept on belting past us, then having a huge broach, we got past again while they were digging themselves out, only to be passed again a few minutes later....until the next broach".

Another memory of these times, and the endurance required to compete in such relatively tiny boats, comes from Roger Geyman, then aged 22 or so, who did the North Sea Race with David Baddeley in another RNSA 24.

"We left Friday morning, and got in on Monday afternoon.... just in time to see all the Class I boats going home. We went on a train to Rotterdam. When we came out of Scheveningen to come home there was a thick fog, so there we were blowing the foghorn every few minutes until someone said 'I don't know what you want to do that for...they won't hear you anyway'..."

Roger's other enduring memory of that race is of the ill-advised purchase of smoked eels which came aboard wrapped in a Dutch newspaper.

Bill Gibbon of Walton & Frinton YC has another memory of a night out in Ostend after crewing the RNSA 24 'Samuel Pepys' which had been chartered from Chatham.

"I got back aboard about 2am and went to sleep" he said "But the skipper got exceedingly drunk and wandered into a Catholic Church, where he took exception to the candles. He had to come back aboard in something of a hurry, and he got the sails up and we got out of the Montgomery Dock. We were five miles out when I woke up. We had no food and no water aboard, and it took us 36 hours to get back to Chatham. We lived on sardines and cheese."

By the end of the decade, two more clubs had joined the Association; the Dabchicks SC from West Mersea and the Royal Temple YC from Ramsgate whose representative W.D. McLennan announced the club would sponsor a new EAORA race in 1959, by which time better facilities would be available in the harbour.

It was also time for a new chairman. Alan Baker retired having served for three years and was replaced by Phil Herring from the Royal Burnham, whose brother Ralph had given his name to the Club's major offshore event, the Ralph Herring Trophy.

Another major player and committee member and supporter from the early years also resigned. This was Geoff Pattinson, a fruit farmer from Gt Horkesley, who was commodore of West Mersea from 1949-1952, and whose trophy the Pattinson Cup is traditionally the Club's first offshore race of the season.

Geoff had a very distinguished offshore racing career, being one of the four co-presenters of the RORC Admiral's Cup, and Captain of the British team in 1969 with 'Fantome'. He was Commodore of the RORC from 1960-2.

Amongst his many boats was the 54ft 'Jocasta' one of the first to be built after the War. Later he owned the 46ft 'Fanfare' designed by Kim Holman, which was twice named as the RORC Yacht of the Year.

The 10th Annual General Meeting was held in Lowestoft at the Royal Norfolk & Suffolk YC. Delegates observed a minutes silence in memory of Donald Spear who had done so much to promote offshore sailing, and had continued to compete in old age, sailing in his beloved 'Brambling' in the Hook Races of 1957, 1958 and 1959 before his death in November of that year.

It was the end of a decade, as well as in other ways, the end of an era. From now on competition would become ever fiercer, crews and equipment more professional and the pressure to do well would be even greater.

Statistics for the 1959 season show that a total of 74 boats raced; with 39 starters for the Pattinson Cup and 25 for the Ralph Herring. Summing up the season in the 1959 edition of "Yachting World Annual" the editor expanded on the summer of glorious weather which had been the best in living memory, making it a memorable season for the lightweather specialists. I quote:

"By far the most popular craft is the auxiliary cruiser. One might almost say ocean racer, for the design and equipment of today's modern cruiser has been so much influenced by ocean racing that any cruising yacht is capable of sailing an offshore or passage race in safety......

Light displacement and reversed sheers now seem to have gone completely out of fashion. Yachts may well be said to have greater beam with longer overhangs and more attention is being paid to proportions and appearance. We have passed the strictly economical and utilitarian stage. Now we enter on a new era of beautiful, functional vessels."

Amongst the other things he noted was that cotton sails were now a thing of the past, with Terylene now de rigeur in cruising and racing fleets; and it was also felt worthy of note that "depth recorders were now being allowed as a method of sounding while racing."

This issue also contained an essay on the development of new types of sailcloth contributed by Paddy Hare, managing director of the West Mersea sailmaking firm of Gowan and Co. who were in the forefront of sailmaking in the Sixties.

Despite the reference to depth recorders, navigation was still more of a black art than a science, and satellite navigation sytems, or hand-held GPS was still far into the future. Radio, as we have seen, was uncertain and there were no such things as wind instruments or speedometers.

In any case few East Coast owners would have gone to the expense of fitting all the latest gadgets when they had always managed by guess and by God, and if it was not always possible that they had correctly rounded a "mark unseen" offshore racing was still an honour sport, where a man's declaration was his bond.

Distance run was measured by means of a Walker Patent Log with its rotating trailer which had to be lifted, read and recorded at hourly intervals.

In very calm conditions skippers still made use of the rudimentary but remarkably accurate "Dutchman's Log" a table by which the speed of travel of a piece of log from the bow to the stern could be computed. This was not just a gimmick.

The author (who worked for Illingworth & Primrose for a heady 18 months or so in the late Fifties, and was called up to crew on Illingworth's 'Myth of Malham' on occasions, including the Fastnet Race of 1959) still has the log of the race in her possession.

This race counted for the second Admiral's Cup competiton, for which 'Myth' was one of the British team, and despite being equipped with every state of the art instrument available at that time, Illingworth issued strict instructions that the crew should consult the Dutchman's Log whenever speed dropped below three knots. A table to work out the speed was permanently pinned up above the chart table.

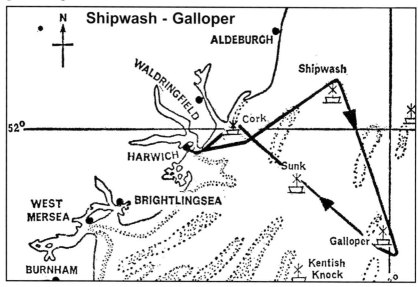

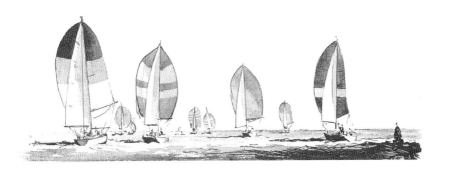

CHAPTER THREE

THE SIXTIES EXPLOSION

"I shall never forget my first offshore race, the spirit of adventure, excitement and achievement continue to this day......."

THE SIXTIES saw an explosion of interest in offshore sailing, and probably the best decade of racing and social life in the Association's history.

Stories of wild races, and even wilder nights ashore are legion. While the old amateur spirit still prevailed, it was no longer enough just to have a boat. As money and materials became easier, new designers were entering the field to meet the more competitive demands of the new breed of racing men.

At the beginning of the decade boats were still built by traditional methods in old established waterfront boatyards. Within a few years the writing was on the wall for wood, as the first production yachts began to appear built from synthetic materials and churned out from factories on out-of-town industrial estates.

On the Crouch boatyards such as Priors, Stebbings, Petticrow, A.W. King and Tucker Brown were working flat out to meet the demand, and the launching of each new contender for racing honours was greeted with celebration and speculation along the waterfront, to a degree which is now totally forgotten, and indeed hardly seems credible.

Boatbuilding and associated activities were the town's main source of employment.

Robin Prior, managing director of R.J. Prior & Son, who still specialise in wooden boat building, remembers the Sixties as an era when his father's yard alone could support a workforce of 160 men.

At the end of the working day hundreds of shipwrights, riggers, engineers and other skilled craftsmen could be seen walking home up the High Street.

The East Coast was lucky in having so many talented designers and naval architects around at this period.

Pre-eminent amongst them was Alan Buchanan, who opened an office in Burnham in 1950.

His timing was spot-on, as offshore racing entered the boom years.

For nearly 15 years the Burnham yards worked all year round producing Buchanan designed racing yachts, all to Lloyds specifications.

Alan spent as much as possible of the season racing, either on clients' boats or his own.

"There was one sure way of developing faster boats, and getting more commissions and that was to win races" he said "We would get three or four orders a month in a good season, mainly for RORC Class II and III boats."

He would also build five or six boats each year on spec.

"If we didn't have an order we'd just start building in September and would always have the boats built by Christmas."

The average build-time was 20 weeks, and boats had to be finished by the end of May for the start of the RORC season.

"On Saturday the owners would come to inspect the progress of their boats, and I used to take them all to lunch at the Royal Corinthian. Often there would be 20 or more of us. Then as the season approached we'd be launching 3 or 4 boats on the same day, and we'd have to run around the yards checking them over. It was sheer chaos."

By the mid-Fifties Alan Buchanan and partners employed

'Taitsing'- Alan Buchanan's 10 tonner

over 20 people, with never less than 12 draughtsmen working and usually more.

Alan won the EAORA championship in 1957 with 'Taeping' a 7 tonner built at Priors. She was followed in 1961 by a 38ft 10 tonner 'Taitsing' with which he won Class I in the 1964 season.

A table of new designs published in the 1959 Yachting World Annual shows that more than 50 new craft were built world-wide. They ranged from one-off state of the art ocean racers to something described as a 'Coronation Day Boat' which was built by Tucker Brown.

His designs were so successful that they made a clean sweep of the prestigious Burnham Town Cup in four of five successive years.

J. Avery's 'Capella of Kent' was the first of these in 1960, and was followed by Ken Trent's 'Vae Victus' in 1961, Maurice Laing's 'Vashti' in 1962 and David Clarabut's 'Vendetta' in 1963.

Following 'Vashti' Maurice Laing had the Olin Stephens designed 'Clarion of Wight' which won both Class I and the EAORA overall trophy in 1966.

Like other rich owners of the time Maurice had no time to  hang about, as John Harrison of West Mersea recalled remembering a Ralph Herring race when there was not enough wind to get home, and most of the fleet were left drifting helplessly with insufficient fuel to reach any destination. "Maurice did not hesitate for a solution" John remembered "A helicopter from the business was summoned with instructions to drop the necessary fuel to enable him to get home." Other Buchanan

'Vashti' - Maurice Laing

successes included Rodney Hill's 'Viking of Mersea' in 1961, and the partially steel-hulled 'Dauber' built at Gt. Wakering in 1964 for R.J.H. 'Bob' Stewart which was to win the Barnard Cup in1966. He also designed 'Noryema' built at Priors in 1958 for Ron Amey, the first of a string of nine boats between 1958 and 1975, all carrying the reversed spelling of his name, between 1958 and 1975.

'Vae Vectis' - Ken Trent, overall winner in 1962 and 1963

Although Ron Amey was part of the British Admiral's Cup team in 1965, 1966, 1967 and 1975 he remained a member of the Royal Burnham YC for many years, campaigning 'Noryema III' under the club burgee during the 1963 RORC season.

These new hot-shot owners, many from the hugely profitable post-war construction industry tended to sweep briefly through the East Coast scene, usually by way of an end-of-season jolly in pursuit of the Burnham Town Cup, but their presence certainly gave East Anglian sailors a taste of serious competition, and perhaps something to aim for as their ambitions grew.

Several became members of the Royal Burnham YC where they gave (and in some cases continue to give) generous financial support to the club, giving rise to the club's quondam nickname "the Royal Builders YC."

One larger-than-life character from this period who did remain mostly on the East Coast, was Ken Trent.

The buccaneering former glider tug pilot, a member of the Royal Burnham, was a generous and popular man, whose exploits were legendary. He and his diehard crew were known everywhere as 'wild men' whose riotous behaviour created mayhem in every port he visited.

In addition to the Town Cup, 'Vae Victus' whose name translates provocatively as "Woe to the Vanquished" brought him the Carmen Cup for Class I and the overall East Anglian championship in 1962 and 1963.

While Alan Buchanan was dominating the design scene at Burnham, a younger rival was emerging at West Mersea.

Kim Holman came from the family engineering firm of Holman Brothers, but by tradition there was no room at the inn for all the sons to find employment, so while Jack went into boat-building at Brixham, Kim followed his naval service by going to work for Frances Jones, the naval architect.

With the help of sailmaker Paddy Hare, Kim later went into partnership with Don Pye and they set up a design office in a corner of Gowan's loft at West Mersea.

The result was a long line of immensely successful East Coast boats.

"He was young and feisty, very generous, and a great enthusiast" remembered John Harrison. "He was a considerable expert, and I learned more with Kim in a couple of seasons than I had in the previous ten years."

The most notable design to come from Holman's drawing board in the early years of the decade was the Stella One Design, whose popularity soon totally eclipsed the then ubiquitous Folkboat.

Some 110 Stellas were built between 1959-1972, mostly at yards on the Crouch, and many went racing where they provided winners for a number of East Anglian trophies.

Kim's first boat won West Mersea's Pattinson Cup on its first outing.

The inspiration for the class came from A.E.'Dickie' Bird, always a supporter of new talent, who commissioned a design for a boat of the same general size and type as the Folkboat but with greater initial stability and increased accommodation below, without frills, which could be built at a reasonable price.

The result was a pretty little clinker-built 5-tonner - 'La Vie en Rose'.

Sonny Cole and George French of Tucker Brown's at Burnham who had already built a number of Holman designs were commissioned to build the new boat, which was to be ready to compete in Burnham Week 1959.

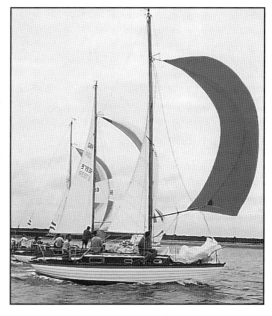

Stella Class - Racing on the River Crouch

As Sonny's brother Bob recounts ".....Like most boat builders we were at panic stations to have her completed on time, and she was only launched two days before Burnham Week started. She was not complete, in that her internal accommodation wasn't finished, but we put all the timber and panels aboard, and she was measured and rated."

Dickie Bird had only two days in which to carry out sailing trials, and his subsequent tally of seven first places in seven days has rarely, if ever, been equalled, and certainly not in a brand-new boat.

The new class was an instant success, but with Tucker Brown only able to turn out 12 boats a year it soon became necessary to replicate the jigs and patterns so that other hulls could be built elsewhere.

During the early Sixties, Stellas were also built by

Petticrows in Burnham, Dan Webb and Feesey at Maldon, Wyatts at West Mersea and Rowhedge Ironworks at Colchester (who also cast all the keels for the class).

The Stellas raced in handicap fleets across the North Sea and the Channel with great success.

Amongst the most notable were two from West Mersea: Rodney Hill's 'Starlight of Mersea' in which he won the overall championship in 1960; and J.A. 'Sammy' Sampson's 'Starshell' which won Class III in 1961 and 1962.

From the Crouch came the unforgettable Freddie Barnes with 'Solaster' in which he won three EAORA events, while class captain Dr Gordon Moore's 'Stella Maia' won a Pattinson Cup.

The exploits of Freddie Barnes, an East London potato merchant and his family were legendary. He owned a number of boats, and the family are popularly credited with having been, at least in part, models for the immortal Giles cartoon family.

Certainly the sketch which showed two small boys in a boat, one rowing away for dear life while the other attacks the bottom boards with a brace and bit, is claimed as a dead ringer for Freddie's sons Peter and Dick.

By 1966 there were 36 Stellas on the Crouch, when Gilly Hedges of the Crouch YC won the Houghton Cup and two other races in 'Lodestar' and David Geaves, of Royal Burnham won the Round the Goodwins Race in his first season with 'Astria'.

The last EAORA race to be won overall by a Stella was the Lowestoft-Harwich Race, which went to Bob Matthews of West Mersea with 'Scorpio'.

In those days the fleet cruised up to Lowestoft and raced back, and John Harrison recalled "...it was a lovely spinnaker broad reach all the way."

By the end of the Sixties the Stellas became superseded by Holman's latest design the 'Twister' which performed better to the new IOR Rule which came into use in 1971. Within a few years

Richard Matthews at the helm of the Stella 'Scorpio' 1958

the Stella would not even have passed muster to race in East Anglian events under the new IYRU Safety Regulations.

That could have been that, but in the Nineties the class has undergone a tremendous revival.

Thanks to sterling efforts by class association secretary Noel Stanbury some 83 of the original boats have been re-located, and many have been restored or rebuilt. They can be found racing in such events as Burnham Week and the Crouch Autumn Series.

It is also good to record that in 1999, in recognition of their 40th anniversary, Phil Mounsey of the Crouch YC did compete with 'Stella Peacock' in the EAORA Jane's Cup, having brought her up to full safety specifications, including a self-draining cockpit.

In a much appreciated gesture he was awarded the Star Trophy at the annual dinner in recognition of his effort.

The 40th anniversary was celebrated with a sail-past of 14 boats during Burnham Week.

Another Stella which still competes regularly in river races is 'Scorpio' now in the ownership of Bob Matthews' son Richard.

'Scorpio' No 9 in the fleet was purchased as a hull and

deck from Tucker Brown and fitted out at home. Today the boat is in pristine condition, having undergone a total refit at Fox's at Ipwich, and is often sailed by a family team in Burnham Week.

With all Richard's other interests, such as his work for RORC, the management of the British Admiral's Cup team, and more latterly his efforts to revive British participation in the America's Cup competition, it is nice to think that he sometimes has time to go back to his roots.

Other early Stella owners, such as Dickie Bird and Sammy Sampson also went on to greater glory in places well beyond the remit of this East Anglian history.

Sticking with the designer who had already done him so well, Dickie Bird commissioned Holman for his 46ft yawl 'Springtime' which went to America to compete in the Bermuda Race in 1961. She was followed in 1966 by the 40ft sloop 'September Song' which like 'Springtime' was built at Tucker Brown in Burnham.

Dickie is always remembered for the way in which he was always willing to find room in his crew to encourage new young talent.

Another fine early Holman design was 'Nymphet' a 26 footer not unlike the Stella, but carvel built, which picked up four first and two second places on her first outing at Burnham Week.

At the end of the week 'Nymphet' was sold to David Brook of West Mersea.

Brook, a war-time glider pilot, had done plenty of sea-miles cruising, but had never raced offshore, and to his own, and everyone else's astonishment, and not a little pique from more experienced competitors, he sailed 'Nymphet' in the Buckley Goblets a few weeks later, and won the race.

His crew for this seriously new learning experience was a rugger playing ex-Army officer Roy Aspinall and Patrick Sixsmith, both of West Mersea.

Brook, whose marriage had broken up, leaving him to cope unaided with the bringing-up of three small boys, thought a boat would be an ideal way to hold the family together.

He wrote about his experiences with 'Nymphet' in 1968 in a wonderful book which should be required reading for all sailing families, and indeed for anyone who aspires to go offshore racing in the North Sea.

By the time "Three Boys in a Boat" was published by Adlard Coles, David had cruised many miles with his young family, including visits to Holland, France and the Channel Islands. He had also been bitten by the racing bug. In 1963 'Nymphet' won the Buckley Goblets for the second successive year, and finished top of Class III to take the Gunfleet Cup for season's points.

A terrifying encounter with a full North Sea gale in 'Nymphet' on passage back from a cruising holiday in Holland eventually convinced Brook that her size, light build, and lack of a self-draining cockpit was a serious drawback in bad weather, and he moved up to another Holman design.

This was the 27ft 'Bandit of Mersea' built at George Cardnell's yard at Maylandsea. Despite her reluctant performance in light airs, she proved to be a potent force to windward in strong conditions, and with her Brook again won the Gunfleet Cup and with it the season's Overall championship in 1965.

Brook wrote about the sea with imagination and passion, including what is probably one of the best descriptions ever written of a small boat struggling to survive in gale force winds as she is almost lost in the treacherous sandbanks of the Shipwash bank off Harwich.

More importantly he proved to himself and to the critics that the family unit could survive; that children relish a challenge and are mostly incredibly resilient.

Brook struck up a close friendship with Ken Trent, one of

those who had been so scathing about 'Nymphet's' first successes on the circuit, and the two families enjoyed cruising in company with 'Vae Victus' in Holland.

Throughout those racing years Roy Aspinall was the backbone of Brook's racing crew, and shared the dramas of the hellish return from Zeebrugge of which he had written so vividly.

The dapper Army captain, who became godfather to one of the Brook boys, started his sailing with Tom Evers the Tiptree builder whose boats included 'Tom Tom' and later 'Diabolo' nicknamed 'The Tiptree Fire Engine' by fellow competitors.

Tom Evers became Commodore of West Mersea from 1961-5, and in the next generation his son Michael was another notable competitor, owning amongst others 'Joe Louis' with which he won the Three-quarter Ton World Cup.

Writing more than 30 years later, as chairman of the Association 1996-8, Roy said "I will never forget my first offshore race, the spirit of adventure, excitement and achievement continue to this day, and are re-kindled at the start of every race...."

Aspinall, another "character" who would come to be known with genuine affection throughout the fleet as "Uncle Roy" and has probably clocked up more sea-miles than anyone else on the East Coast, owned a succession of boats.

"Always second-hand" he insists, without rancour "I've only ever had other people's boats. You've got to remember that after the War we were all looking for jobs or a career, and we had young families to bring up and school bills to pay. We were all doing it on a shoe-string."

His first independent command was a Yachting World Lightcrest, which he describes as "a funny little boat which fell over all the time."

This was followed by a 5.5 metre 'Venus' in which he enjoyed many battles with David Geaves and 'St George'.

He later purchased Stella No 1 'La Vie en Rose' from

Dickie Bird, and this was followed in due time by the North Sea 24 'Mar del Norte'.

The North Sea 24 was another Holman design, intended as a rival to Alan Buchanan's East Anglian One Design, of which the prototype was 'Whiplash' built by Tucker Brown in Burnham for millionaire Dick Wilkins.

Later 'Whiplash' was owned for

'Cervantes IV' - Triumphant Admiral's Cup team 1971

many years by the Herring family of Burnham, and both veterans were still around in the Seventies when the Libya Cup for the Beta Division went to Aspinall in 1974, and to the Herrings in 1975 and 1976.

Another well-documented North Sea 24 was 'Andorran' owned by David Edwards, which John Harrison sailed to victory in the 1965 RORC Channel Race.

Holman also designed 'Fanfare of Essex' built in 1964 by the Berthon Boat Company in Lymington for Geoff Pattinson, and 'Cervantes II' built at Priors in Burnham in 1965 for Bob Watson, on which Brian Foulger, a future chairman of EAORA, sailed as watch leader.

Watson was another owner with a tradition of retaining the

same boat name. His 'Cervantes IV' sailed for the British Admiral's Cup team in 1971, under the burgee of the Royal Burnham YC.

Superseding the Stella, as we have seen, Holman's next major production success was the Twister.

'Twister of Mersea' built in 1964, was campaigned through most of her first season by John Harrison.

To his great delight they won the East Anglian championship, despite losing the mast in one race.

Recalling the incident John said "It was the same year that Bernard Hayman (for many years editor of Yachting World) launched 'Barbican' in Class II. They passed us on the windward leg, and then we caught up with lots of other boats including 'Barbican'. We were grinding up through her lee, and the genoa had gone a bit saggy, so we heaved on the 'tweaker' (a four-part tackle positioned between the two standing backstays which Harrison and Holman had devised to put more curve in the mast) and the mast fell down."

"Oh what an unfortunate occurrence" - he remembers was the only comment, coming from Paddy Hare.

Bernard Hayman (irreverently known in the fleet as 'Haybags') was not a great racing man, but his long distance cruising exploits in 'Barbican' were well documented in the magazine, and he was always a tireless campaigner for the use of proper safety equipment, as well as a lecturer and examiner in the disciplines of marine radio. In the 1990's he was honoured in recognition of more than 20 years service as an Auxiliary Coastguard.

Another well-remembered Twister was 'Cheetah' campaigned by Harry Croker of the Crouch YC who took the overall championship in 1967 and 1968.

Besides Alan Buchanan, Burnham could also lay claim to another yacht designer, in Guy Thompson, an amateur with advanced ideas, who was one of the first to promote the fin and skeg profile. As his ideas developed he produced a series of nine yachts, all called 'Calliope'.

David Geaves remembers this boat as being "very innovative, built of plywood, multi-chine with a sloping cockpit floor and the famous opening 'back-door' in the transom, an idea which came to be widely copied."

Thompson's best known design was probably the T24,

Dick Pitcher helming 'Goosander'

commissioned by Dick Pitcher of the Royal Burnham in 1965. Dick was then a world class dinghy helmsman, but he asked Guy to draw him the lines for a small cruiser.

The result was 'Goosander' a 24ft five-berth cruiser which in 1968 became the prototype for the production model T24.

While never quite as successful on the racing scene as the Twister, the T24 became extremely popular as a family cruiser, and a number are still around today.

Having parted with 'Goosander' Dick Pitcher bought her back in 1977, when the author's eldest son Andrew survived his offshore baptism by fire in the Buckley Goblets of that year.

"It was one of those years when most competitors were forced to leave their boats behind and come home on the ferry" she remembers "as any other anxious Mum I was very concerned about them until 'Goosander' having sailed back with just the two of them on board popped up in the Crouch quite unfazed and wondering what all the fuss was about!"

Thompson also drew the lines of a T25, of which only two were ever built. Peter Duce of the Crouch YC who sailed with Jasper Blackall on 'Huckleberry' can still recall the domestic trouble which resulted when the antique candle-burning lamp which they had borrowed to hang on the forestay as a riding light as they lay off Shotley Point on the night before a Harwich-Ostend race, fell overboard as they were getting it down the next morning.

Thompson's next design, also for Dick Pitcher, was the T31ft 'Williwaw', a lineal descendant of the T24, but actually very different. She was the first British designed and built Half Ton Cup boat to sport a trim tab and bustle, which brought her a clean sweep of points in the EAORA Class III in her first season.

Towards the end of the decade another new design blazed a trail across the racing scene. This was the Hustler, which in its various conformations was to become one of the most successful designs ever seen.

It started in 1967 with John Harrison's Hustler 28 'Catalana' a fin keeled racer cruiser built in plywood by Nick Canerias in Spain.

According to John who met him when he came to Gowans to buy sails Canerias was an eccentric Hungarian Count, who claimed to be a direct descendant of Genghis Khan, who had flown Messchersmitts for the Luftwaffe in the Second World War until captured by the Russians. He subsequently fetched up in Canada where he worked for Westinghouse and became acquainted with the American yacht designer Rod Stephens. Fired with enthusiasm for offshore sailing he returned to Europe and set up a boat-building business in Spain.

The next boat he built for John was 'Gunsmoke' a modified 28 which won the Harwich to Ostend race followed by an overall win against a large fleet in the Ostendebank race.

John loved to race competitively and half-way around the course for the Houghton Cup that year - which was still a night race - he offered the crew a free dinner for every yacht passed before the finish. All through the night John was literally bubbling with enthusiasm, and by the time dawn broke there were 40 yachts astern.

The crew ate free for a long time, but John's company Island Boat Sales was very much up and running.

Encouraged by this John moved from one-off building in Spain to series production in fibreglass in the UK with the Hustler 30, which was built by Leslie Landamore in Wroxham, who until that time had only been involved in building boats for the Norfolk Broads.

The Hustler 30 was an instant success. Built for the incoming IOR rating rule they proved to be potent performers, especially against the S & S34's which had been built for the previous rule.

The first 'Seasmoke' was sold to Peter Clements of West Mersea. John's second 30 was 'Ricochet' which was skippered for the Fastnet Race by Richard Matthews with an almost all Mersea crew including Peter Clements and 'Tubby' Brook (whom we have met earlier in this chapter with his father David in 'Three Boys in a Boat').

John won Class III and was overall champion with 'Ricochet' in 1971.

A series of other Hustler models followed inluding the 35,

John Harrison 1979

and the 25.5 of which the first UFO was lent to Richard Matthews "to see what he could do with it" and by 1974 John could claim that Hustlers, in various versions, had won five East Anglian championships since 1968.

In 1976 John, ever the innovator, commissioned a relatively unknown designer Stephen Jones to build a 32 footer to the half-ton rule.

'Zaviera' built as a wooden prototype by Landamore's was rocket-ship fast. She was shipped to Australia for the Sydney-Hobart but structural problems forced an early retirement. Nevertheless the new Hustler SJ32 became the boat to beat in the 1978 Half Ton Cup, and others followed including the 36, 30 and 27.

Amongst them was 'Bright Spark' built for Rodney Hill which was modified and given a bigger rig. 'Bright Spark' was later owned by Terry Swann who won the overall championship in 1980, and later still by David Powell who won the Class II Trophy in 1982.

John was not only a successful builder and racing yachtsman; he was also a serious seaman, and a skilled engineer.

At the age of 61, with his son Paul, he joined the crew of the 43 footer 'Storm Bird' which was dismasted in heavy weather, 1200 miles out of Bermuda. For one night they lay ahull, streaming the broken mast as a drogue, and then erected the stump as a jury rig. They sailed the remaining 2000 miles to the Solent, unaided, at an average speed of over 6 knots. For this feat the whole crew were presented with a special RORC award for outstanding seamanship.

In 1990 at the age of 72 John joined the crew of 'Crusader' for the 12 metre European Championship in Holland not as shore support as one might expect, but as mainsheet grinder!

Only a year before his death, and with health problems, he sailed from Fiji to Auckland, a 1500 mile passage of which 1000 miles were hard to windward in a full breeze. He never missed a watch and earned the respect and admiration of everyone aboard.

A keen fisherman, wild-fowler and countryman John was a man of all seasons, and a wonderful story-teller. He also served West Mersea YC for more than a decade as sailing secretary, inaugurating their RNLI Pennant Race and the club's Autumn Trophy.

As one of his shipmates remarked " To share a night watch with John was to open an encyclopaedia on sailing and on life."

Another notable yacht from this period was Dr Nick Greville's Holman & Pye designed 'Trocar' built by E.C. Landamore in Wroxham in 1969. After more than 30 years of continuous competition, both in EAORA and RORC events this classic partnership must have a good claim to having sailed more miles than any other East Coast boat.

It is recorded that when Dr Greville inconveniently found himself the owner of two boats at the same time he made history by skippering 'Trocar' on the West Mersea-Ostend race, while his wife Shirley skippered the 30ft Rustler 'Scalpel' in the same race with an all-female crew. 'Trocar' holds the distinction of being the best placed East Anglian boat in the Fastnet Race, having come third overall in 1975.

I am grateful to Dr Greville for early information about the part played in the Association and the RORC's affairs in his history of the West Mersea YC published to mark the club's centenary in 1999. Indeed it would be difficult to underestimate the contribution made by the club's sailors to the general development of offshore sailing at this period when they achieved the ultimate accolade of winning the RORC's Martin Illingworth Inter-Club championship no less than four times, in 1954, 1964, 1967 and 1968.

While West Mersea was picking up honour and glory elsewhere, other member clubs came to the fore in the Sixties. The inter-club trophy was won five times between 1960-6 by the Royal Burnham, and by the Crouch for the first time in 1967 and again in 1970.

The Royal Burnham's finest year was 1961 when they were placed fourth in the RORC inter-club championship, and won both major East Coast team events the Amazon Cup and the Nore Command Cup.

The individual championship for this year was won by 'Lora' (David Edwards, D.M. Cuthbert and L. Bromley) who with 'Vae Victus' (Ken Trent) and 'Taitsing' (Alan Buchanan) comprised the victorious Royal Burnham inter-club team.

'Lora' was a remarkable boat, and given that she was then celebrating her fiftieth season, her inclusion in the team was

'Lora' - Successful cruiser racer in 1934

something of a record. The 30ft sloop, designed by J. Pain Clark was built by W.A. King in Burnham in 1911, and had been raced in many EAORA events by Ralph and Phil Herring before coming into the ownership of David Edwards and Leslie Head, also a lawyer.

Another regular member of the crew was Joan McKee, whose culinary skills were much appreciated. Joan later became a long-serving secretary to the Association in succession to the Buchanans, holding the job from 1968-73.

David recalls "Nobody believes that there is such a thing, but when we bought 'Lora' in 1956, we were all impoverished young lawyers. We got her for a very good price thanks to the kindness of Phil Herring. She had nothing at all, no log, no speedo, no Beme loop or anything like that, except a second-hand grid compass which we bought from an Army surplus stores for about 30 shillings."

"We had this boat which we didn't really know anything about, and I don't think we had ever done anything except perhaps a couple of East Anglian races when we entered for the RORC North Sea Race in 1957. When we came out of Harwich it was a dead beat to the West Hinder, and taking the tide into account we set off on the port tack. Everyone else went off in the other direction. After about two hours we couldn't see anybody at all. When the tide turned we tacked. We didn't see anybody all night. But when we got to the West Hinder there was 'Lutine' and 'Myth of Malham' and the other big boats, but not a sign of anyone in our Class III. We put up our great big penalty spinnaker to run off up to the Smith's Knoll, and we made jolly sure we kept in touch with the other boats as we hadn't the faintest idea of how far away it was. We came round Smith's Knoll with the Dutch yawl 'Tullia' a lovely boat which was very fast and we raced with her all the way into the Hook, and somehow we eventually managed to squeeze ahead of her. We won the race overall, our very first RORC race!"

David continued his story: "......It wasn't altogether well received, and when we got up to the Royal Maas in Rotterdam everyone came on board. They simply couldn't understand how we had got ahead at the West Hinder when we had 'gone the wrong way' at the start.

They were quite indignant when we pointed out that we had taken advantage of the tide, and someone told me 'You don't want to worry about the tide, you want to race against the other boats!'. 'Listening to the advice you get from old hands is usually unhelpful; they have their own reasons' he concluded dryly."

David also recalls with some affection the first boat in which he raced with the East Anglian fleet in 1953, and with which he had again incurred the wrath of some of the senior competitors of the day. The boat was 'Fiesta' a plywood centre-board design which he built himself, in partnership with Leslie Head of Royal Burnham.

"Mersea was cock of the walk then, and the Pattinson Cup was one of the top fixtures of the season. It was our first race. We set off down the Wallet to the N.E. Gunfleet and as usual the tide was the crucial factor, and by the time we got to the buoy the ebb was starting to run.

'Angel' - David Edwards helming at start of Burnham-Hook of Holland Race, 1972 Force 8

But 'Fiesta' only drew about 2ft 3ins with the plate up, so we were able to go right in over the sand and crack up inside everyone else. The Gunfleet buoys were not marks of the course in those days. but Alan Baker, commodore of West Mersea thought we had been a bit cheeky, and he was absolutely furious. We did win the Pattinson Cup, but there was a good deal of disapproval..." he chuckled.

Recalling the same race Leslie Head remembers that Dick Pitcher was supposed to be part of the crew, but had not appeared by the time they had to leave the Quarters. Eventually he was put on board by a club launch, to take the tiller still wearing the previous night's dinner-jacket.

After 'Lora' David's next boat was the North Sea 24 'Andorran' purchased from John Harrison in 1964 which he owned in partnership with his brother Eric (Lord Chelmer) winning the Barnard Cup for Class II in 1965.

After this the lure of the South Coast took him away from East Anglia for a number of years, although the next boat 'Angel' designed by the American Dick Carter was built at Tucker Brown's in 1968. She turned out to be a wonderful light weather boat, and is well remembered for a string of successes in Burnham Week in the hands of Tucker Brown's senior partner 'Sonny' Cole.

In 1969 David became Commodore of the RORC, and it was during his term of office that the International Offshore Rule (IOR) was introduced to British ocean racing, being used for the first time in 1971.

This was also the era when the RORC finally shook off its image as a relaxed 'gentleman's club' (with the cheapest overnight accommodation in London) and metamorphosed into the highly respected national authority which it is today.

In the early 1990's David was also instrumental in promoting moves to find a One Design offshore racer which would be more affordable for those without long pockets than the constantly changing one-off's which sought to exploit every nook and cranny of the IOR system. But he never forgot his early days on the East Coast with EAORA, and in 1975 he returned to take over the chairmanship in succession to David Clarabut of the Medway, winning the overall championship in the same year with 'Hylas' a Dick Carter design built in 1973. David later became Admiral of the RORC, succeeding Sir Maurice Laing, another former East Anglian supporter, but he still looks back with affection to the Sixties.

"Those were really the absolutely peak years" he said. "Afterwards nobody wanted to stay out all night, and all they really wanted to do were Burnham Week type races."

Although strictly speaking the RORC North Sea Race does not come within the remit of this history, it enjoyed support from East Anglian sailors for many years, even if the points did not always count towards EAORA season's trophies.

The rot only really set in with the divergence of rating systems, and an increasing reluctance amongst the smaller boats to embark on a gruelling 200-mile slog across the North Sea. Even the application of 'bonus' points could not re-activate its appeal.

As the principal RORC event on the East Coast the race has always been one to separate the men from the boys, and carries a heavy burden of myth and legend based both on the habitually foul weather conditions, and the hospitality and exploits at the Royal Maas YC's post-race party.

Another factor tending to lessen its appeal was the decision to hold these celebrations at Scheveningen. This may have saved competitors a tedious 16 mile haul under engine upriver to Rotterdam, but it also helped to encourage others, short of time at the end of the weekend to spin on the line and return home instead of going ashore in the smartest dress they could achieve which was part and parcel of the old ethos of the race.

In its hey-day the North Sea Race was preceded by the RORC Southsea-Harwich Race a feeder to bring competitors round from the South Coast. Hosted by the Royal Harwich YC who erected a large marquee on their lawn, the pre-race party was always a memorable thrash.

One competitor, recalling the Fifties told me the party always got off to a good start with the arrival of a deputation from the Navy at HMS Ganges bearing two pint jugs of duty-free gin.

"How the Hell we ever got down to the start the next morning I do not know" he confessed.

The start was from a line off the Pier Hotel at Harwich, with the Guard buoy some 500 yards ahead as the first mark, at uncomfortably close quarters for swift action from crews still nursing sore heads from the previous night's party.

The Southsea-Harwich fixture did not survive long past the Sixties, in the face of competition from other events in the ever-growing yachting calendar, and the all-too-real dangers of racing yachts through the busiest shipping lanes in the world past Dover.

The reality of these dangers was forcibly brought home in 1971 when the Dutch yacht 'Merljn' was run down with the loss of all six members of her crew during the North Sea Race. Following the accident David Edwards, by then Commodore of the RORC, decreed there would be no more racing in the Channel to the East of the Royal Sovereign light vessel, or in certain parts of the southern North Sea.

The decision was not well received on the East Coast. Writing in the RORC's house magazine 'Seahorse' in December 1971 John Harrison, a regular contributor of East Coast race reports, described the decision as "a bombshell." These were waters, he pointed out, in which the Association had been sailing for the last 21 years, and in their view, the situation was "not as bad as all that."

"The organising clubs will continue to review courses in the light of changing conditions, as they have always done," he declared. "In fact, shipping into the Thames has declined and in the approaches to ports such as Harwich, where it has increaased enormously, ships are moving relatively slowly and keeping a look-out. There will continue to be cases of collision at sea, but these seem to happen even out on the oceans, and surely cannot be considered sufficient reason for us to stop racing in our home waters?"

Although the Southsea-Harwich Race was never revived, pressure from the East Coast eventually led to the introduction of a second RORC race. This was organised by West Mersea with a finish alternating between Breskens and Nieupoort, and was seen as a useful second qualifying event for those wanting to join the RORC. It also became a regular East Coast fixture for the Level Rating Championships which became a feature of racing in the Eighties. But, as racing grew more professional throughout the Sixties cracks were beginning to appear in the organisation, and especially in the management of races, which were the responsibility of the individual sponsoring member clubs.

This could, and did, get difficult from time to time, as competitors grew more demanding and less willing to tolerate inefficiences of any sort. The East Anglian committee were kept busy trying to persuade part-time club secretaries and sailing committees to get their house in order.

The problems even surfaced in the press, when in 1968 after muddles over the rating of one entry Anthony Churchill wrote a scathing denunciation of race management in EAORA in the July 11th issue of "Yachting and Boating Weekly"

"While RORC and JOG organisation cannot be foot-faulted, EAORA is still tripping over its own success. This gallant series of races wins the popularity prize, but swelling entries are not matched by improving organisation.

The root of the problem goes deep. It is the yacht clubs themselves who banded together to form the Association - the clubs themselves run the individual races and their efficiency varies from the excellent (the Crouch YC) through the mundane to the unacceptable. There is a central organisation run on a shoe-string, employing a part-time and overworked honorary secretary. The task of the honorary secretary in trying to tell each individual club what it should do must be back-breaking."

He concluded "The lesson is simple. If clubs cannot organise individual races then radical changes in EAORA are needed. An organisation closer to the RORC structure should be the aim, where it is individuals who join, it is individuals who fill the coffers, and larger cash funds should be used to employ a permanent secretary who can round to each start or finish and hold the hand of the organising clubs. An East Anglian Paul (*Author: Alan Paul much loved RORC Secretary of the day*) is required. East Anglians you have nothing to lose by protest."

In November of the same year the same publication (and

probably the same writer) reported from the AGM, raising concerns which were always in the forefront of the Association's mind, as it endeavoured to reconcile the needs of its sharp-end competitors with those of keen, but less well-heeled competitors.

He wrote: "Two key-notes were sounded. First there is a growing disquiet at the rapid obsolesence of racing yachts. No sooner are they built than designers dream up some other shape to out-sail them. With the New World Rule looking large around the corner (the Introduction of IOR in 1971) obsolesence will increase. Many yachts built for the RORC rule may be outmoded at one fell swoop by the IOR Rule.

With this in mind, EAORA has taken two steps...... They are to split the fleet into 'A' and 'B' so that old timers may still have a chance of picking up the 'B' prizes. This brings EAORA into line with the RORC. But EAORA is taking the matter a pace further. While the RORC has brought in an age allowance bonus on the TCF, EAORA is to add to this with another bonus of its own."

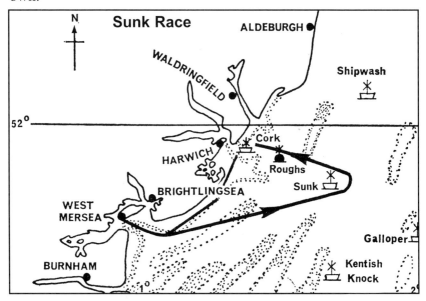

CHAPTER FOUR

TED HEATH and OTHERS

"After racing it brought everyone under the same roof for a pint of beer and an argument......for me, this has always been one of the joys of sailing"

THE ARRIVAL of the S & S34 in 1969 created something of a watershed in offshore racing history, although their history more properly belongs to the Seventies, when for a while they dominated the scene, and were the boats that everyone else wanted to beat.

At the end of the Sixties, as racing faced up to the introduction of the new IOR rating rule designers grasped the chance to develop ideas, many of which would become prototypes for later production models. This would in turn lead to boat-for-boat racing, classes within classes, and eventually the Level Rating competitions. The S & S34, from the American designers Sparkman & Stephens set new standards and revolutionised expectations of windward performance. They became classics, and quite a few are still around, and still giving a good account of themselves in the new Millennium.

Once it became known that the Leader of Her Majesty's

Opposition, and later Prime Minister Edward Heath had ordered a boat, there was no holding the class. Offshore racing - usually the most misunderstood and poorly reported branch of sport, was suddenly 'Hot News' - blazoned on the front pages of every newspaper. Journalists struggled to explain to their mystified readers the attraction of sailing. An even more difficult concept for the general public to grasp were races when crews might actually spend the night at sea.

Even more impenetrable for the average readers were the intricacies of a handicapping system under which the last boat home could easily turn out to have beaten those already home and dry an hour beforehand. Politicians and Press thundered about the risks involved, the security of the Minister, and the problems and international repercussions that might arise from his being even temporarily out of contact with the shore.

The prototype S & S was the One-tonner 'Morning Town' built in wood by Mike Winfield, which some claim has never been bettered. The production 34's many of whom continued the 'Morning' prefix were moulded from fibreglass. Many were finished off at Prior's yard in Burnham. They included: 'Morning Jade'; 'Morning Glory'; 'Morning Flame'; and 'Morning Melody'. Probably the best known was 'Morning After' built for Rodney Hill of West Mersea who later went on to purchase the original 'Morning Town' from Mike Winfield.

Mike Spear's 'Monday Morning' was built in 1969. " She cost £6,750 new from the yard" he recalls. But he only kept her for 2-3 seasons, realising that the design was already becoming superseded.

Another S & S built in the early 70's for Peter Clements of West Mersea became the first of many successful boats to carry the name 'Carronade'.

Inevitably the focus of interest was on the first 'Morning

Cloud' built at Mike Winfield's Medway yard for Edward Heath, then Leader of the Opposition Conservative party. Heath had only taken up dinghy sailing some three years earlier, but became hooked on offshore racing when Maurice Laing took him on the RORC's Dinard Race in 'Clarion of Wight'.

He was looking for a boat of his own when he visited the London Boat Show and was immediately impressed by the accommodation below decks of the new S & S34. Heath describes his sensations on first seeing the boat in his autobiography "Sailing. A Course of my Life" published by Sidgwick & Jackson in 1975. He was particularly taken with the teak finish, which included the cabin sole, and "gave an air of stability and well-being."

'Morning Cloud' was launched in April 1969 and her first offshore

'Morning Cloud' - Ted Heath at the helm

race was West Mersea's Pattinson Cup, for which Heath's crew was joined by the designer's brother Rod Stephens. The proud new owner was totally won over by Stephens meticulous approach to tuning, and race preparation, and was even more delighted when 'Morning Cloud' won her class, and was only narrowly beaten to the overall honours by David Powell's 'Mersea Oyster'. It was an encouraging introduction to the sport in which Heath was to play a major part throughout the 1970's.

Under the leadership of Owen Parker, Heath's crew for the

first season included several East Coast sailors. Amongst them were Anthony Churchill, then a member of the Blackwater Sailing Club who was to become the regular navigator, and Anthony Law of the Royal Burnham. Another who became part of the crew was 'Tubby' Lee, the professional rigger of Burnham.

'Morning Cloud' did enough EAORA races in her first season to take the Barnard Cup for Class II. Later, as more ambitious plans matured to take 'Morning Cloud' to Australia for the 1969 Southern Cross Series, the crew were joined by Sammy Sampson from West Mersea and Duncan Kaye from the Royal Corinthian. Sammy was a wonderful sailor who sadly died early.

"Every boat that Sammy touched was always well sailed, with good technique, skill and dash" remembers Roy Aspinall "He was a dedicated man, and as hard as nails."

The British team for this Southern Cross Series included Arthur Slater's 'Prospect of Whitby', Max Aitken's 'Crusade' and Rodney Hills 'Morning After' - 'Morning Cloud' was named as reserve boat.

It is a matter of record that Heath became the first British skipper since Captain John Illingworth RN to win the Sydney-Hobart Race, and had her score been added to the team instead of being reserve boat, the team trophy would also have gone to Gt. Britain.

With his second 'Morning Cloud' Heath went on to captain the British Admiral's Cup team in 1971, and what is perhaps even more remarkable, while holding down the office of Prime Minister, he also won the coveted Roman Gold Bowl as the overall victor in the 'Round the Island Race' in three successive years between 1970-73.

Sammy Sampson and Anthony Churchill (at that period the editor of the RORC magazine 'Seahorse') were in Australia again in 1972 with the second 'Morning Cloud' another Sparkman &

Stephens design built by Clare Lallow in Cowes, this time as an official member of the British team for the Southern Cross Series. She won her class in the Sydney-Hobart Race, and only an ill-timed hole in the wind some 40 miles from the finish prevented the crew from bringing home the double. Another East Coast competitor in Australia in 1972 was Dickie Bird with 'Morning Town'.

Although Ted Heath's subsequent racing career was mostly

'Morning Cloud'

on the South Coast, he remained faithful to his early East Coast connections (and to his constituency at Broadstairs) with regular visits to compete in the Ramsgate Gold Cup (which he won twice, in 1969 and 1974) and to Burnham Week where he won the Commodore's Cup in the first 'Morning Cloud' in 1970, and the Town Cup in the second 'Morning Cloud' in 1972. He always retained an affection for the East Anglian scene.

"After racing it brought everyone under the same roof for a pint of beer, and an argument about what had gone wrong (or occasionally right) and a continuing discussion about everything affecting small boats and those who sail them. For me this has always been one of the joys of sailing" he wrote.

Sadly it was on the return trip from one of these expeditions to the East Coast in September 1974 that the third 'Morning Cloud' was lost at sea, claiming the lives of two crew members including that of Heath's god-son Christopher Chadd.

Brian Foulger (EAORA Chairman 1978-81) was amongst the first East Anglian sailors to go for the new S & S34, as a replacement for his American-designed Rhodes Ranger 'Ailish'.

"They were wonderful boats, 'Ailish' was the fourth S & S to be completed at Prior's in Burnham" he recalled. "Upwind they would sail themselves better than any helmsman, but downwind if you didn't look out, they broached all over the place." Thirty years on 'Ailish II' is still going as well as ever, and is based at Largs in Scotland from where in recent years she has circumnavigated Ireland, Scotland and the British Isles with her current owner.

There are dozens of tales relating to the "hazards" attendant on having a VIP politician in the fleet. Brian Foulger recalled one Burnham Week, when there was a change of course just before the start. "There were four S & S34's in the fleet. At the South Buxey most of the fleet carried on, but while we (Ted Heath, Arthur West and Brian Foulger) peeled off on the correct course, the police boats who were supposed to be following 'Morning Cloud' didn't spot what had happened and went straight on. Our course, which was the correct one, was rather longer, and when we got back there was a major panic going on because the Prime Minister's boat was missing."

Relating the same incident in his book Ted Heath recalls that Rodney Hill and 'Morning Town' was the first to take the wrong course, and set their spinner for the return leg up the river, while 'Ailish' which was always well sailed and a keen competitor and 'Morning Cloud' both sent 'dummy' crews up to the foredeck with the spinnaker turtle to fool Hill into thinking they were about to follow suit!

On another occasion Brian Foulger recalled that the policemen detailed to keep watch over 'Morning Cloud' on her mooring off the Royal Corinthian YC momentarily left their post, only to find when they returned that the Prime Minister's boat was missing.

She was located on the scrubbing hard at Priors, where an indignant Tubby Lee, who was only following instructions to scrub the bottom was all but arrested on suspicion of taking the Prime ministerial yacht without consent.

"Oh we had some fun, one way and another" Brian recalled. He particularly relished the occasion when 'Morning Cloud' came alongside at the start of one 150 mile North Sea Race to ask if 'Ailish' could spare some food. Somehow in the heat of the moment the stores had not been put aboard, and the PM and his crew faced a long and hungry passage.

But it cannot have been all fun and games trying to race with a Prime Minister in the fleet, not least for the security services detailed to look after him or for the media seeking a good story. There are even those who would argue in retrospect, that Heath's influence on offshore racing was less than benign. He certainly helped to put offshore racing on the map, and made it better understood and appreciated.

But the unseemly scramble to jump on the social bandwagon and to be seen competing in the latest fashionable activity, undoubedly helped to distort the pace of change beyond its natural growth.

The pressures hastened what one might call "the end of innocence" and the old Corinthian spirit, as it pushed offshore sailing beyond the means of ordinary sailors, especially on the East Coast which has never shared the prosperity and conspicious consumerism of the South Coast. As big money, big competition and professionalism in the form of hired hands came into a previously grass-roots activity, the pressure to keep up became an impossible burden for even the keenest owner.

"Heath put offshore racing on the map, but at the same time he spoiled everything. Nothing was ever the same again. There was huge media interest, and pressure to beat him" said Harry Bird of Royal Burnham "Before Heath came along we used to race with the boats we had got, and even if you didn't have the best sails or the most up-to-date gear, you could still win if you got the navigation right.

It was still fun. There were all these rich men, and you knew you couldn't beat them, but you could all still have a drink together in the bar after the race.

When the new rules came in (IOR introduced in 1970) there were all these designers coming up with the latest experiments and go-faster ideas, and it just became too expensive. Successful owners who had perhaps expected to have a new boat every two or three years, just didn't have the money, especially if they had young families to bring up, so they gave up and decided to do something else."

Harry was a regular member of the crew of George Farmer's very successful 'Mereva' and also of 'Lothian' where things were still done in the old ways, and the old attitudes to crew comfort still prevailed.

"We always had food aboard - good North Sea stew. George knew we would all go better with a hot meal inside. We had young crews sometimes whose eyes were on stalks when they realised there was food to be had. Some of them had never had a meal cooked on a boat before" he said.

George was on the point of building a new boat to replace 'Lothian' when the new IOR Rule was introduced in 1970. He became so disenchanted by the new design frenzy that he concluded he could no longer afford to compete on level terms.

'Lothian' was given up, and George became a motor-boat man, cruising widely with his beloved 'Olivebank' (named, so it was claimed "half for his wife Olive, and half for the Bank"!)

He never lost his interest in offshore racing, or ceased to support the Association, and in the Eighties he generously provided 'Olivebank' as the committee boat for the first, and several subsequent Race Weeks.

Another regular competitor who saw the light at this stage was Mike Spear. He was then racing 'Maleni' the first big boat to be built by Eversons at Woodbridge in 1962. The firm subsequently built 'Golden Samphire' for Sammy Sampson, and several Twisters.

Mike was successful in 'Maleni' taking the Barnard Cup for Class II in 1964. She was also a regular visitor to Holland for the Flevo Races.

"I couldn't afford to buy a new boat every year, so we decided to stick with what we had, and just do the best we could with an old boat" he said.

After 'Maleni' came the UFO 'Obsession'; a Contessa 32 and a Contessa 35 'Moonboots' but none of them ever had such a hold on his affections as the Swan 'Moustique' which he still owns, and describes as "the love of my life."

Mike has crossed the Atlantic on several occasions, raced in Cork Week and in many of the longer RORC races to place such as Bayonna and La Rochelle, but surprisingly he has never done a Fastnet. "I cannot see the point of sailing 600 miles just to finish up in Plymouth" is his considered view.

'Moustique' is still raced in Haven Series events by Mike's son-in-law Alan Major, where she continues to give a good account of herself in all weathers.

David Geaves is another who holds strong views about the professionalism which began to creep into racing in the Seventies.

"There was never anything wrong with professionals being part of the crew. What was different was when people began to be paid to steer. The character of the sport completely changed. It has never recovered and I don't think it ever will."

Prime Minister Ted Heath was not the only notable figure in world sailing to make his mark on the East Anglian fleet in the 1970's. It is not generally remembered that the New Zealander Peter Blake (now Sir Peter Blake and one of the world's most experienced blue-water ocean racers) had some of his early racing experience in the UK.

Once again I am indebted to Faith Tippett, editor of West Mersea YC's newsletter 'Moliette' and to the author, the late John Harrison for permitting me to reprint this article, entitled "Knight's Gambit" which appeared in March 1996.

"Crump...swoosh, the boat had just come off a big one, when through a veil of spray running off the peak of my cap, I became aware of the upper half of a face, framed in the opening left by the top missing gap-board. Level blue eyes, a firm forehead and lots of blonde hair. The voice, pitched just high enough to carry above the cacophony of wind and wave, had that softer of the two Antipodean accents, becoming increasingly familiar to us British yachties.

"Ah, John" it said "Bloody chicken in the ice-box. Shall I cook it ?".

Now the culinary disposal of a domestic fowl would not normally be a subject for much surprise or comment, but this was a bit different. We were off the Wolf Rock, Number 2 and a reef, beating into a biggish sea - and 35ft cruiser-racers in those days were proper yachts which carried their sail well!

But perhaps I should go back to the beginning of this little story. In 1970 we had raced 'Midas', Dick and Barry Pearson's new Hustler 35 to Ostend in the EAORA race from Harwich, planning to carry on down to the Solent for the RORC Cowes-Cork Race.

Whilst giving myself the statutory heachache that goes with the so-called beer served in the North Sea YC bar I was approached by old mate and sailing adversary Harry Croker who had brought his Twister 'Cheetah' round from Burnham for the race.

"Johnny" says Harry "Got this young Kiwi with me, name of Pete, knows what he's doing. Wants to go down to Cowes for a look round. Can you take him?"

"Sure Harry" I says "Glad to." Harry beckons over this tall blonde young man whose six-foot four disguised a powerful flat-muscled build, giving a first impression of lankiness.

Pete had very little to say for himself, but after a bit of probing I learned that he was 19, and had arrived in England with a letter of introduction from Gilly Hedges with whom he had been sailing back home in Auckland in Gilly's Sparkman & Stephens one-tonner 'Escapade'. Before emigrating to New Zealand Gilly had been Stella class captain at the Crouch YC, hence the connection to Harry Croker.

Pete joined us aboard 'Midas' and we sailed next morning on passage South. After the rigours of the Ostend apres-sail the crew were a touch sluggish as we motored out through the pier heads into the usual roly-poly jumble of sea.

Pete volunteered to get the gear on so we could start sailing, and by the time we were under sail I knew that we had aboard a pearl of a seaman beyond price.

Pete hooked on the gear dead right, whilst walking round the decks seemingly impervious to the violent motion, and apparently blessed with suckers on his feet!

The passage was uneventful apart from a not unusual August fog bank in the **Straights**. We were somewhere near the East Goodwin, outside the sands, when from the direction of Ramsgate there came the sound of rapidly approaching high speed engines. This had Pete worried (it was the only time I saw Pete worried at sea!) as from the chart I had pointed out the unseen Goodwins which were drying.

I knew it was the recently introduced Hovercraft service, but didn't let on. Pete's eyes opened wider and wider at the thunderous approach until out of the mist burst the big SR2 with its four props whirling, to pass close across our stern.

The lad had never heard of a hovercraft, so the experience was a bit unnerving!

To complete the crew for the Cowes-Cork Race we were joined by Don Pye, the boat's designer and quite the best race navigator and strategist with whom I have had the pleasure to sail. Don and myself were, and are, mates of very long standing and we were anxious to see how 'Midas' would respond to this first serious test of offshore ability.

It would take too long to describe the race, so suffice to say that we got a good start, and with St Alban's Head abeam we had the clutch of S & S34's, our deadly rivals, well astern. EAORA were well represented with 16 yachts from the East Coast, including five from West Mersea.

Conditions were mostly about heavy air to windward, and so we came to be west of the Wolf Rock when Pete dug out the chicken, and posed the "Shall I cook it?" question.

Anyone who has tried cooking a full roast meal in the galley of a 35 footer bucketing to windward in Force 5-6 will know that this is not easy, requiring an iron stomach, miraculous sense of balance, and the patience of Job.

Apart from the peas momentarily developing wanderlust,

Pete managed it superbly and those of us who fancied it (and by now there were those amongst us who definitely didn't!) were able to jam themselves somewhere strategically in place and tuck into the roast chicken, peas and mashed potato all topped off with a very passable gravy.

For myself, after a long spell at the helm, this intake of good hot grub did wonders, heightening further my respect for our Kiwi wunderkind.

However good Pete was in the galley, he was even better on deck; throughout that long windy beat whenever I found myself thinking "We're a bit pressed. Should we go down to the No. 3?" Pete, as if mind-reading, would appear with a cheery "Want the No. 3 on, John?" and would stride forward and hand those big flogging sails as if they were a dinghy's. It was just the same when the time came to change up.

The EAORA boats made their mark in that toughish race, somewhat to the chagrin of the hot South Coast contingent. John Boardman's big 'Border Law' won overall, 'Midas' took Class IV humbling the previously all-conquering S & S34's by a huge margin, and other East Coast boats were well in the prize lists. They included Guy Clarabut's 'Akela' from the Medway which won Class II.

Once ashore at Crosshaven in the hugely welcoming Royal Cork YC Pete displayed another talent by hammering out on the long suffering bar piano such Antipodean masterpieces as "Waltzing Matilda" and "Wild Colonial Boy" etc. Memories of the run ashore seemed to fade after that... I wonder why?"

Pete returned to West Mersea with John, and stayed for several months becoming virtually part of the family, and sailing many more hundreds of miles.

"In recent years he was kind enough to say that I was a good master" John recalled "All I can remember teaching Pete was that bare feet on North Sea Races were not a very good idea!"

Pete left the Harrisons to join Les Williams' 72 footer 'Ocean Spirit' (then the largest fibreglass yacht ever built) for a passage from Malta to the Cape. On this delivery trip, which became something of a saga, Pete acquitted himself so well, and became so indispensable that on arrival in Capetown, Les was only too pleased to waive the fee he had originally demanded for a berth on the Capetown - Rio Race.

This was the first of the big Trans-Ocean races, and it is nice to think that but for John Harrison and the EAORA the blue-water racing bug might never have bitten the young Peter Blake!

John's story concludes:

"One Clement Freud was ship's cook for that Rio race, and I remember him telling the story in a television interview how much of his best work would have been wasted but for a certain Pete who was always ready to go through anything set before him, regardless of the weather and the indisposition of most of the crew!"

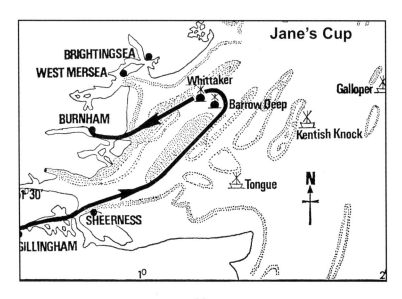

CHAPTER FIVE

ALL CHANGE IN THE SEVENTIES

"We must have had a good week because three of the couples aboard got married..............."

THE EARLY Seventies were hailed by Jack Williams (Chairman 1969-72) as "the most successful in the Association's history in terms of real achievement, both within the Association, and in the activity of its members in the ocean racing world in these, and other, waters."

It was certainly a period of all-change on the racing scene. Most important was the introduction of the IOR rating rule, which at a stroke changed the fortunes of many older boats.

Committees spent many hours debating how to come to terms with new developments and to promote new ideas without losing the essential character of the sport.

It was clear that EAORA would have to come into line with RORC, and they somewhat reluctantly adopted the new Rule for the 1971 season, while agreeing to differ over class limits, which would have resulted in a huge and unwieldy Class II.

Essentially it was the same old problem, of keeping the

hot-shots happy whilst not discouraging older designs, and more traditional cruiser/racers. To keep these competitors happy a Beta Division was introduced. Harry Pye of Royal Burnham donated a huge silver trophy, the Libya Cup, for the 1970 season to which were attached a complicated set of conditions and age allowances.

The committee now agreed that boats built before 1966 should qualify for a one per cent deduction from their TCF, while those built before 1963 should take two per cent. Medallions were also offered for the first three boats. Age allowances were a nightmare, not only in the Beta division, but throughout the fleet where the more technically minded (or those professionally affected by the success of their designs) indulged in endless argument.

Should for instance, a boat's age allowance be dated to when she was built; or back to the design date. What should be done about subsequent modifications to the hull shape, or sail plan? Optimisation was the name of the game.

There were endless anomalies, which continued to be a subject for contention until 1978 when the Association finally agreed to adopt IOR Mark III(a) with a TMF time allowance.

Every aspect of racing was becoming more professional, and as we have seen in Chapter 3, endless grumbles were provoked by sloppy time-keeping and administration by some of the clubs.

A new Points System was also needed, to iron out other anomalies which had arisen during the Sixties. The basic problem was the impossibility of ensuring an equal spread of points using a system based on the number of starters, when popular races offered double the points available on less well supported occasions.

Although by rule of thumb it was accepted that "by and large the right winners had emerged" the system clearly operated in favour of the top boats, and did not give adequate reward to those middle of the fleet competitors who sailed a lot of races with moderate success.

As an experiment bonus points were offered for three races in 1967, to see if this evened things up a bit.

By 1971, after extensive research by John Harrison and Peter Clements, the Association agreed to adopt the Cox-Sprague system. This had been in use for some years by the MORC in America, and offered points down to 80th place. The new system gave greater emphasis on 4-13th places, thus helping the 'triers' and favouring boats which did a full season. It also had the great virtue of being easy to understand.

At the end of the season the overall championship went to John Harrison with 'Ricochet' and if proof of the success of the new system was needed it turned out that David Brook's 'Matambu' had not only won the Beta Championship, but had also beaten many more modern boats to win Class I in the Open Division.

Delegates to the 1971 meeting had two other major matters on their minds. These were the 125th anniversary of the Royal Netherlands YC to be celebrated during the 1972 Flevo Series; and nearer home, the threat to yachting amenities on the East Coast from proposals to build for a third London Airport at Maplin.

Environmental and 'green' lobbies were only in their infancy, but the idea was widely felt to be an intolerable threat to the area. If the Maplin Sands had not been so remote, wet, and so well guarded by the Experimental Weapons Establishment based on Foulness Island, or so devoid of suitable vegetation for tree-dwellers, there would undoubtedly have been Greenham Common-type stake-outs. No 'Swampies' arrived to camp out, but local communities were outraged by the proposals.

Apart from the noise and disturbance it was widely feared that the massive land reclamation work to accommodate runways would have a catastrophic effect upon long established navigation channels and swatchways, and would totally disrupt maritime activity of all sorts. Every organisation from the Royal Yachting Association to the Dengie Hundred Preservation Society had their own ideas about how the threat should be tackled.The Association added their weight to the protests by appointing Brigadier Basil Chichester-Cooke as their spokesman to the RYA.

Although the Flevo Races were never part of the East Anglian season they come into our story at this point, because of the number of EAORA boats which regularly sailed over to Holland to support the event during the Sixties and Seventies.

One of the major attractions was the team race between Dutch and English boats for the Cannon Ball Trophy, which as we have seen in an earlier chapter was inspired by Brigadier Chichester Cook. The team was composed of three boats, sailing three races over three days.

I am greatly indebted to David Cole of the Medway Yacht Club, now the Trustees of this trophy, for an account of the Flevo Series in 1966 when he competed in his Kim Holman designed Twister 'Brigand Chief' (still racing in 1999, and recently sighted in Antigua!).

"As Class IV RORC she was too small to be part of the Cannon Ball team, although she had won many races in the EAORA and four main trophies.

The best crews had been wooed aboard the Cannon Ball yachts, but my wife Pat and I were fortunate enough in securing the services of a husband and wife, both elderly but experienced.

The Flevo Races attracted a very large attendance. Starting from Muiden they included passage races to Enkhuisen, Hoorn, and back to Muiden.

Before becoming landlocked the Isjelmeer was the Zuider Zee and was almost fresh water. In fresh winds hundreds of small fish would be sluiced along the decks through the scuppers.

The first race from Muiden took place in glorious conditions and we finished in second place. The second race from Enkhuisen started in very hot, light air conditions. The whole fleet became becalmed. As there is no current there were no kedges. After an hour the sails were black with thunder flies.

The day wore on, no sign of a breeze. Suddenly the sky went black. Then came torrential rain and force 7-8 wind. The Flevo Races had never finished in the dark before. The buoys were very small and navigation had to be accurate. We managed to find the last mark before heading to Hoorn and the finish.

Unfortunately our navigator forgot to take a log reading at the last mark, so how on earth in such conditions could we find the finishing line? After half an hour I looked astern to see the navigation lights of a Class I yacht slowly catching us. As he crept past his stern light revealed his name 'Witte Raffe of Hoorn'. "Well," I said to the crew "If anyone knows how to find Hoorn he must! Up spinnaker! We can't afford to lose him."

The demand nearly caused a riot, but up it went and we just clung on. Eventually a searchlight pierced the blackness and picked up the Dutch yacht's sail number. He immediately rounded up and dropped his sails. The light then covered us, and as the Dutch yacht moved off I took a compass bearing on him, and we followed the same course.

The next day the clouds were hurtling over the rooftops of Hoorn. We lay next to a Dutch yacht. "Surely they are not going to send us out in this?" we asked our neighbour "In Holland, whatever the weather we go out" was his response.

The race officers, ensconced on the commodore's large motor yacht, called an hour's delay on the loud hailer. On the hour, to our surprise, our neighbour prepared for sea. It was all we could do to set storm jib, fully reefed mainsail and get to the line by the five minute gun. But the short steep seas did not trouble the heavy displacement 'Brigand Chief'; she revelled in the conditions, unlike the unfortunate race officers whose motor cruiser could not reach the finish line in time! Fortunately the commodore's brother who was the leading yacht in Class I saw his predicament, dropped anchor, took his own time and hoisted a string of flags to mark the line and timed in every yacht.

The wind was so strong the water had been blown downwind from Muiden YC and we had to be towed up the last few feet of the canal to get alongside. After two hours a notice was put up on a post near us, and a crowd of those tough yachtsmen they seem to breed in Holland surrounded it.

Peering over their shoulders, very few yachts seemed to be listed. "Where are the rest of the fleet?" I asked. One large specimen looked down on me "Do you think we Dutch are so bloody stupid as to be racing in weather like this?" he responded.

"So that is how 'Brigand Chief' became the first foreign yacht ever to win the Flevo Races."

In 1971 the series was won by the East Anglian team of 'Xuxu' (David Barham); 'Puffe' (Leslie Landamore); 'Fleetwind' (R.Brooks) and 'Morning Jade' (Ron Holland) sailing against a very strong Dutch team, and a field of 220 boats.

The following year the team comprised 'Sootica' (Sammy Sampson); 'Mar del Norte' (Roy Aspinall) and UFO (Richard Matthews).

The trophy was won for a second time in 1978, but there is no record of the team.

Brian Foulger who took part in several of the series remembers "They were great fun. We had some marvellous times over there."

One year when the East Anglian entrants included Brian's 'Ailish', Peter Clements 'Carronade' and Basil Chichester-Cooke with his Nicholson, the team hired a motor cruiser to accommodate the ladies and the spare crew. "We must have had a good week because three of the couples aboard got married, including my daughter, and they have all been successful!"

Although participation in the Flevo Races died off in the late Seventies, the series still exists, although without such a large international contingent. Since then several attempts have been made to involve our two countries, notably in some of the the East Anglian Race Weeks in the Eighties, without notable success.

At the time of writing (the 2001 season) it is hoped that English yachts may participate in two days of the Flevo Week races during EAORA Week, and there are also plans to revive the Cannon Ball Trophy with a team race from Ostend to Breskens.

As numbers steadily increased in the early Seventies the Association had plenty of cause for optimism. In 1971, for the first time, entries reached the magic mark of 500, of which 108 had raced in the Beta Division.

During the season 121 boats had taken part, of which 34 were Beta types. Racing was as keen as ever, despite bad weather, and all the major trophies remained undecided until the last race.

The club championship went to West Mersea, and overall to Leslie Crawley with 'Nenno' while John Gozzett won the Beta Division with 'Shaker' which was also runner-up in the Class II Open Division.

The Class III championship went to Richard Matthews of West Mersea with 'UFO' one of a new generation of Hustler's which were to dominate the scene for the next few years. Richard, as we have seen in Chapter Three, sailed with his father Bob in the Stella 'Scorpio' after a childhood spent messing about in dinghies. His first command, at the age of nine, was a Yachting World pram dinghy built by his father.

His first offshore experience came at the age of eleven

when he was invited by Tom Evers of West Mersea to crew aboard 'Viking of Mersea', a clinker-built Alan Buchanan design.

"I went along as working crew. I always smile when I think of that because the idea of asking an 11 year old to go on a 50 mile offshore race sounds a bit bizarre" he said.

In the early 70's Richard crewed for a number of owners, including two or three Admiral's Cup trial races with David Powell on 'Mersea Oyster' and for Rodney Hill in the original S & S 'Morning Town' which he had purchased from Mike Winfield. He sailed with John Harrison on 'Gunsmoke' and later 'Ricochet' when she competed in the Half Ton World Cup.

In 1970 John suggested they should get together to promote the new Hustler 25.5, designed by Don Pye and built at Landamore's in Norfolk.

In 1972 in his first season as a skipper Richard campaigned 'UFO' finishing first in class, and second overall. At the end of the year he bought the boat from John Harrison, fitted her with a three-quarter fractional rig (just coming into vogue at that time) and proceeded to win Class III for the second time, and the EAORA 1973 championship with her.

With this success in hand Holman & Pye were commissioned to design a slightly larger boat which became the Ufo 34. Richard made a licensing deal with Colvic, and the fledgling firm of Oyster Marine was in business.

He remembers "The first Ufo order I signed was in a Wimpy bar in Witham, since in those days we had no office."

The boats could be purchased fully fitted out to the highest standards by Leslie Landamore of Wroxham, or in various package forms for completion elsewhere, and the concept proved to be incredibly successful. By 1976 Richard could boast that the Ufo 34 had outsold all other competitors put together in the UK.

In the Association's handbook for 1977 his advertisement

'Mersea Oyster'

for Oyster Marine listed all the owners who would be racing new Ufo 34's in the coming season, with the previous designs they had now disowned. They included Michael Spear, Peter Clements, Geoff Holmes, David Cassidy, Mark Fellows and Don Pye, Chris Brooke, Alan Bartlett, Monty Lockwood, Robert Ballantyne, Colin Grundon, Bob Stewart and George Thake. Thirty years later the Ufo 34 is still around on the East Coast.

Richard's original boat became the redoubtable 'Bellerophon of Mersea' under the ownership of Captain Roy Aspinall. Since those days 'Bellerophon' has become another East Coast legend, having covered more sea-miles in bad weather than most other yachts with 'Uncle Roy' and his long-standing crew of intrepid (and now geriatric!) reprobates. It is recalled that when 'Bellerophon' lost her bowman over the side at the start of one race, the average age aboard dropped by twenty years.

'Bellerophon' was finally sold in the late 1990's having given a very good account of herself, including many voyages undertaken in the service of largely disabled crews. Another veteran Ufo 34 still around on the scene, and now introducing a third generation of 'Coppernob' youngsters to sailing on the Crouch is Arthur Galloway's 'Scarlet Streaker'.

West Mersea was undoubtedly the dominant club in the Association throughout the Seventies, winning the inter-club trophy for an unbroken run of thirteen years between 1971 - 1984. (Over the first 20 years six different clubs had put their name on the coveted trophy).

Amongst the notable West Mersea sailors of the period were David Powell with a succession of boats including 'Mersea Oyster' (originally the Dick Carter designed 'Rabbit II') with which he tied for the overall championship in 1970 with George Blake's 'Golden Dragon'.

David's early career with his father's 'Naiande' and Alan

Baker's 'Thalassa' have been touched on in an earlier chapter, but he is another long-standing supporter of the Association whose contribution cannot be over-estimated.

Following 'Naiande' he owned 'Galloper' designed by Buster Brown which he sailed in the 1964 Fastnet, coming second overall, as the youngest skipper in the race.

His Fastnet record is remarkable. In 45 years he has competed in 21 races, only missing two events, and he was amongst those who took part without mishap in the infamous 1979 race. Amongst his most regular crews is Ken Newman who has been aboard for almost all these races.

In 1969 he accompanied Rodney Hill to Australia for the Sydney - Hobart Race in which they came fifth, and in 1975 he went back to Dick Carter's design board for 'Mersea Pearl' with which he was one of the British team who took their boats to America for the Onion Patch series.

Other successful West Mersea owners who cannot be omitted from this roll-call included Jock Smith with 'Tumblehome' overall champion in 1977 and 1978; and Frank Reed with 'Tramp' who was champion in 1979 (and is still going strong twenty years later).

Class winners included Rodney Hill ('Morningtown'); Sammy Sampson ('Sootica'); Peter Clements ('Carronade'); Ralph Struth ('Silver Shadow'); Ron Wigley ('Mumbo Jumbo); Ralph Dreshfield ('Mukluks') and Alan Hill ('Mischief of Mersea').

Another innovation of the Seventies was Level Rating. Introduced by the RORC, possibly as an attempt to sort out all the problems of ratings, this was a competition in which boats of differing design but similar rating could race boat-for-boat.

The first series for Three-quarter Tonners was held in 1973, when two East Anglian races were included as qualifying events.

The move helped to boost local entries in the RORC's two East Coast fixtures, and there was great local pride when the series was won by Peter Clements with 'Carronade'.

Level rating was an exciting new concept, but it was not easy to fit it into a normal East Anglian season. For a start there were not enough entries to split the fleet into the five classes specified by the Level Rating Association.

Committees were much exercised about the best way of integrating the new concept with its crew limitations, safety factors and other regulations. But no harm could be done by having a level rating division within the usual set-up.

In 1974 International Yacht Paints agreed to sponsor a Level Rating Series within the East Anglian, and to provide points trophies in the one ton, three-quarter, half ton and quarter ton level.

Five of the season's races were nominated, and competitors could choose from the Ralph Herring, the Thames Estuary, the Houghton Cup, the Shipwash-Galloper, and the Round the Goodwins events. The two RORC races were also included.

The biggest take-up within the East Anglian fleet was in the Three-quarter ton class where at the end of the season the chairman would congratulate Bob Stewart of Royal Burnham in achieving a third place in the World Championships sailed in Miami.

The Level Rating competitions brought in new competitors, especially in the smaller divisions where Adrian Jardine and John Mullins of British and European Boat Sales in Burnham became specialist builders of Quarter-tonners.

Their most notable production boat was the 'Robber' another which could be built in wood or grp and made available part-built or complete.

In 1974 Mike Richardson shattered the claims of all the larger boats when he carried off the EAORA overall championship

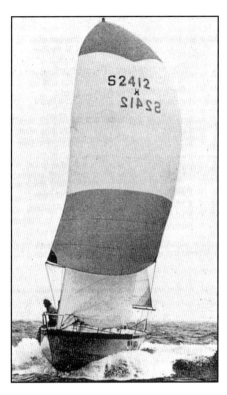
'Robber'

with 'Runaway Robber'. His record included first place in the Sunk Race, the Lowestoft-Harwich and the Buckley Goblets. He also achieved seven first places in Burnham Week.

In 1977 a new season's trophy was added to the EAORA programme. This was the Gozzett Cup for Class IV which was won by the Jardine twins, Stuart and Adrian in two out of the first three seasons. Along with other initiatives, like the Beta Division, to encourage more traditional sailors, came the Star Trophy. Originally known as the Crouch YC's Maximum Points Cup, the trophy had become somewhat superfluous, since it almost always went to the overall winner.

David Barham's suggestion that it should be awarded at the committee's discretion for the most meritorious unrewarded performance, or service by a yacht during the season was accepted.

Always difficult criteria to assess, the cup has been awarded for a few examples of good seamanship, but has usually gone to the dedicated but unsuccessful 'hard trier'.

The first recipient was Bill Chapman who had competed in all 12 races for the previous two seasons, and had been unsuccessful apart from one class win.

The following year it went to Roger Chadney, owner of 'Stardust' then the only Stella still racing offshore regularly. It was noted that he had competed in the Buckley Goblets in gale force conditions with only one girl crew. In 1976 it went to Charles Chapman of Royal Burnham with his home-built 'Autumn Breeze'. Other early recipients included John and Bridget Watkinson of the Royal Corinthian who completed every race in the 1981 season except for one, in which 'Golden Silence' lost her mast.

Len Baker of Royal Burnham completed 12 out of 13 races in 1983, while J. Green did 14 races in 'Hud' in his first offshore season. In 1987 Roy Aspinall received the cup, 'Bellerophon' having been the only Channel Handicap yacht to complete all the races for the Royal Thames Championship, and in 1988 it went to James Mattison of RBYC with 'Prairie Oyster' who won his class in the RORC Plymouth-La Rochelle Race.

Jonathan Leggett of Haven Ports YC was honoured in recognition of his fine seamanship in coming to the aid of a Belgian yacht off Zeebrugge in 'Chimp'.

In 1999 the 40th anniversary of the Stella Class the trophy went to Phil Mounsey who competed in the Jane's Cup with 'Stella Peacock' the only remaining yacht to comply with safety regulations.

After 25 years in 1974 the Association was ready to celebrate its Silver Jubilee. The great social event of the year was the first Chatham dinner. The venue was a bonus, resulting from a disastrous fire in February 1973 at the Royal Burnham which had been expecting to host the dinner.

Thanks to Basil Chichester-Cooke's efforts Brigadier John Purser of the Royal School of Military Engineering at Chatham agreed to allow the dinner to take place in the magnificent setting of the Royal Engineer mess at Brompton Barracks.

It was a notable honour, and the first occasion on which any outside body had been allowed to hold a function there. Numbers were limited to 150. It was a black tie affair, with an orchestra and the 5 course meal with a pre-dinner drink, wine, and liqueurs was priced at £4.50.

Following the annual general meeting held at the Medway, the diners were transported to Chatham, where they dined with great magnificence on Potage de Tomato a l'Orange; Mousse de Merluche Fumee; Cote de Porc en Croute, and Creme de Banane aux Amandes.

The programme of music included Viennese Melodies by Lehar; 'Nights of Gladness'; 'Destiny'; a selection from Cole Porter's 'Can Can' and the tango 'Jealousy'.

But the memory which probably remained most vividly was the precision with which silent-footed Army servants performed their ritual removal of the table-runners, twisting them into a tight roll the length of the table, which could be whisked away on an invisible signal.

The Association were again honoured to be allowed to dine in the mess in 1983, and 1990, but plans to celebrate the centenary of the Royal Engineer YC in 1996 with another EAORA party had to be dropped for security reasons.

Nevertheless any East Anglian sailor privileged to have dined there at any time will never forget the occasion always made even more luxurious by the offer of overnight accommodation and a full English breakfast for survivors!

It seems appropriate to conclude this chapter with another very special East Anglian occasion.

This was the race up the Thames organised to celebrate the Jubilee of Her Majesty the Queen in 1977. The Ralph Herring Trophy was diverted to finish at the Medway on the weekend before to act as a feeder, with a staggered start from Garrison Point

The Jubilee Race up the Thames - Left to right: 4321 'UFO' (Richard Matthews); 4069 'Heatwave' (David Cassidy); 3627 'Dingo' (David Cole); 4116 'Golden Sovereign' (John Gozzet)

on the following Saturday May 21st for the 42 mile trip to St Katherine's Dock.

On reaching No 2 buoy in Woolwich Reach yachts were instructed to start their engines and motor through the Thames Barrier until they reached No 8 buoy.

I am greatly indebted to David Barham of RHYC (Chairman 1981-84) for the loan of his Race Instructions for this event, which are illustrated with some delightful pen and wash sketches of St Katherine's Dock, Trinity House and of the church of All Hallows Berkyngechirche by the Tower where the Vicar, the Rev. Peter Delaney held a Service of Thanksgiving by Yachtsmen on the Sunday morning for 25 years of the Queen's reign.

The occasion was graced by the trumpeters of the Royal Engineers YC, and the congregation included the flag officers of all the London yacht clubs and organisations concerned with the maritime life of London.

Welcoming his congregation Mr Delaney said "Ever since King Charles II brought his yacht 'Mary' to London, and moored her within sight of this church, a strong and active link has continued between our British monarchs and British yachting, that has become part of our sea heritage, and is as strong today as ever."

"..........It is fitting that yachtsmen should come to London this year, and to this Church, to offer thanks for the twenty-five years of this Reign, for All Hallows has been closely connected with those who go down to the sea in ships for more than a thousand years."

In mediaeval times the tall spire was a navigation point, and also the sign that another voyage was over. Many great sailors have prayed here, and it is worth recording that Sir Francis Chichester began his epic voyage on his knees in All Hallows."

David Barham has added a pencil note to the order of

service which reads "This event was dreamt up by Basil Chichester-Cooke and largely organised by him." It was the sort of grand gesture to be expected by so ardent a traditionalist and supporter of the Association.

The last event of note in the Seventies was of course the notorious 1979 Fastnet Race, which brought death and tragedy to many including a number of East Anglian families.

The most terrifying experience of many was that endured by the crew of the Crouch Yacht Club's entry 'Trophy', an Oyster 37 designed by Holman & Pye and owned by 53 year old Alan Bartlett.

After being rolled over and dismasted the eight men took to their liferaft, which after a number of capsizings and rightings, to their horror suddenly split without warning into two sections, leaving those in the upper half clinging to what was effectively no more than a rubber ring.

In the struggle to survive, two men were swept to their deaths, and a third died of exposure before they were picked up. When the remaining men were rescued the following morning they were more dead than alive having been in and out of the water for more than eight hours.

Another East Anglian boat which played a prominent part in the rescue operation was Rodney Hill's ketch 'Morningtown' from West Mersea which was acting as the RORC's official escort vessel, responsible for monitoring radio channels.

Despite being herself disabled when the steering gear failed, 'Morningtown's' crew did a sterling job in keeping race headquarters in Plymouth in touch with the situation as it developed.

Six French crewmen also had cause to be grateful to David Chatterton of West Mersea when they were hauled aboard 'Moonstone' after abandoning their yacht.

Other East Anglians who sailed in the race and came through relatively unscathed included David Powell; Fiona Wylie who sailed on the Contessa 32 'Ascent', and Brian Foulger of Royal Burnham.

On being questioned by an importunate reporter in Plymouth after the race, it is recorded that this modest and much loved man, with his usual masterly understatement, would only admit "It was a bit choppy!"

A full account of the race was given by the American writer John Rousemaniere in his book 'Fastnet Force 10', (*Published by W.W. Norton & Co 1980.*)

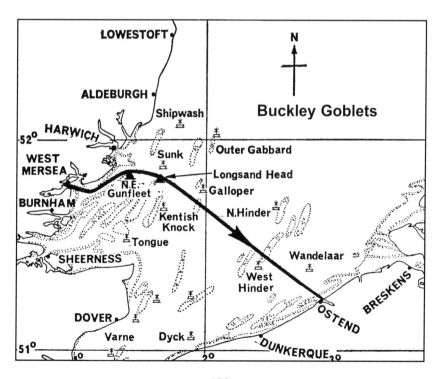

CHAPTER SIX

THE EIGHTIES: Stopping the Rot

"It all went wrong in the Eighties.....everything had to change...."

THE EIGHTIES began on a slightly down-beat note. In his 1980 report chairman Brian Foulger noted it had been a bad year for tides, the weather had been poor, and the Pattinson Cup had been sailed in the coldest conditions anyone could remember.

Entries had begun to slide from the high point of 511 in 1978. The greatest loss was from Class I where there had been only one starter in the Houghton Cup, and none at all for the Sunk Race. Small boats were on the decline, with only a few completing the required number of qualifying races in Class IV. As much as anything this reflected the reluctance of owners to make long delivery trips between races.

By 1983 starts for Classes III and IV would be amalgamated where there were less than five entries. Even in Ostend, where the notorious 'hook finish' was a perennial bone of contention, two owners had been hauled before a Belgian court for failing to observe harbour signals properly.

Nevertheless, Terry Swann, the overall winner for the season, had competed in all 13 races in 'Bright Spark' and competition in Class II was on the up. The runner-up was John Harrison with 'Gunsmoke' and third place went to the Class III 'Santa Evita' (Tubby Lee and Terry Vernon).

West Mersea had won the inter-club trophy for the 12th time in 13 years, but the gap was closing. Royal Burnham were within 400 points!

One bright hope for the future was an East Anglian Week. This, as we shall see in a later chapter, was not a new idea, having originally been mooted by David Cole of the Medway as far back as 1969. In 1979 it was raised again by Ian Marks of Blackwater SC who thought it might fill the gap left by the defunct level rating competiton.

Another new initiative came from the Royal Thames YC who offered to sponsor an East Coast Championship, mainly with the aim of encouraging support for the two East Coast RORC races. The series would include three of the most demanding EAORA events. The first championship was held during the 1981 season, but was somewhat spoiled when two-thirds of the fleet were forced to retire owing to exceptionally bad weather for the West Mersea-Zeebrugge Race.

For the following season the Royal Thames came up with three extremely handsome and historic trophies. The King George V's 1st European International Yacht Race Cup, 1911 would go to Class I; Lord Queenborough's Cumberland Cup to Class II; and the Empress of Russia's Jardiniere to Class III. The club also provided glassware for each class. On the first occasion these magnificent and valuable trophies were presented at the Association's annual dinner, but unsurprisingly it was not long before the club ruled that the trophies could no longer leave the London clubhouse.

Although as we shall see in Chapter Seven the first East Anglian Week in 1982 was a great success, but overall entries were again down. The average entry for each race had fallen from 54 to 43. This decline was not by any means confined to the East Coast. Similar tales came from other areas, and it was a time of national economic depression. But it was cause for concern.

Looking for some sort of solution, Richard Matthews, the season's overall champion with 'Oystercatcher', drew attention to the increasingly successful Haven Series. This was run under the Portsmouth Yardstick Sytem, a considerably cheaper and less onerous rating system than IOR, which might appeal to the less serious owner. It was not the first time the Association had considered holding an additional class for non-IOR boats, but the idea had always been shipwrecked by the practical difficulties of setting a different or shorter course for one class, as well as by the traditional system of allocating the major season's prizes for overall, rather than class results.

Another joker in the pack was ORC Special Regulations, Category III, which were adopted in 1983.

While no-one could argue the importance of carrying the proper safety equipment the requirement to carry a liferaft was a considerable cost and liability for smaller boats, such as the Robber class. At the other end of the scale, others pushed for Category II, arguing that races across the North Sea did not, strictly speaking, come within Category III, which covers races mostly in sight of land.

At this point it was finally decided to relax all restrictions on electronic aids, which had hitherto prevented competitors from using the increasingly affordable and available Decca navigation system.

In many ways the declining support was hardly surprising. Only the most determined and well heeled competitor could hope to cope with such a demanding annual programme made up of 13 races, most of which started and finished at different places, and required extensive logistic support by way of delivery trips and crew shuffling.

The tendency towards bigger and bigger boats, requiring ever larger crews, was another factor. It was also increasingly difficult to persuade competitors to support races at the periphery of the area, such as Lowestoft or Dover, where racing was no longer practicable in the congested waters of the Channel, and port facilities anything but welcoming to yachtsmen.

By 1986 the race for Royal Cinque Ports YC's Prince of Wales Cup was dropped from the programme, while the Royal Temple YC concentrated on forging closer links with their French neighbours. Another scheme was the 'Back to Back' weekend, reducing the burden by doubling up two races into one event.

Walton & Frinton YC's Walton Trophy and the RN & SYC's Lowestoft - Harwich went together like a horse and carriage, but there was considerable opposition to a shot-gun marriage between the Royal Corinthian YC's Thames Estuary Race and the Medway's Jane's Cup.

At this time the Medway Race did not finish at Garrison Point, but carried on up-river to Upnor, a long slog often in falling breezes against an ebb tide, which did not endear itself to competitors, particularly when they faced a return journey the next morning.

A third 'double' matched the Friday night's Shipwash Race with a short day-race for the Sunk Trophy on the Sunday.

But there were some plus points. Thanks to the persistence of chairman David Barham of Royal Harwich, the 1983 annual handbook contained, for the first time, sailing instructions for all races in the season. The move ended a long tradition of inconsistent and sometimes badly drafted instructions issued by the sponsoring clubs, which had frequently caused problems on the water.

The only casualty of the new approach was the pleasing tradition of little sketch maps of the course which had decorated the pages of earlier handbooks. (*Author: Some of which I have used, and which were revived, I am delighted to say, in the late 1990's*)

Entries for the 1983 season were again disappointing, some 20 per cent down on the previous year. More alarming was that many fewer than usual had completed the six races needed to qualify for season's trophies. The drop was particularly acute in Class IV where only one yacht qualified, and in the Beta Division there were no qualifiers in either Class I or IV. The overall winner for the second year in succession was Richard Matthews with the latest Stephen Jones designed 'Oystercatcher'.

More remarkably perhaps, considering the disparity between them, the runners up were Mike Holmes and Tony Allen with the much modified 1979 vintage Humphreys half-tonner 'Harmony' by a short whisker from Tom & Vicky Jackson's classic Swan 'Sunstone'.

The season was also notable for the duels between the two Sigma 36's campaigned by Peter Clements 'Carronade' and David Chatterton 'Aquatracka' who finished first and second in Class I.

The Star Trophy was awarded to Len Baker of Royal Burnham, who had entered all 13 races, completing 12 of them.

Despite all these underlying difficulties, the 1983 season ended in a blaze of glory when the Association was once again permitted to hold the annual dinner in the magnificent surroundings of the Royal Engineer YC's Brompton Barracks at Chatham.

One of the first actions of the new 1984 committee was to appoint Peter Clements, John Harrison and the East Coast measurer Joe Isaacs to look into the RORC's newly introduced Channel Handicap Rating System, which it was felt might be the basis for a new non-IOR division.

There was a sudden burst of enthusiasm in Class I with the appearance of two well-known South Coast One Tonners in their new incarnations as 'Ark' (The Oyster 43 ex 'Black Topic' chartered by Tim & Cathy Herring) and 'Big Boots' (ex the Rogers designed 'Yeoman'). They would find plenty of competition from John Wiltshier's fire-breathing 'The Red Dragon' and John Oswald's brand new Hugh Welbourne designed One Tonner 'Sidewinder'.

Despite all these new rock-stars in the East Anglian firmament,

'Sidewinder' - (John Oswald) 1984

and despite a trip to the Baltic and an appearance in the Three-quarter Ton World Cup Richard Matthews' all conquering SJ 35 'Oyster-catcher X' captured the overall championship for the fourth year in succession, against strong opposition from her sister-ships which included Ron and Malcolm Struth's 'Silver Spirit' and Kit Hobday's 'Erotic Bear'.

Mike Holmes and Tony Allen continued to rule the roost with 'Harmony' in Class III, and Rory Macnamara, a

'The Red Dragon' - winning at Burnham Week 1984

commercial pilot and highly ingenious navigator from the Royal Burnham put up several fine performances with the elderly 'Scampi' running rings around many a hot-shot rival amongst the sandbanks.

Numbers also held up reasonably well with 531 starters in 15 races, and a total of 86 boats came out to play. There was one other almost cataclysmic result - After a run of thirteen years the inter-club trophy was finally wrested from West Mersea by the Royal Burnham YC. It was also the end of another era, as at the annual dinner at West Mersea competitors took leave of the auditor Brigadier Basil Chichester-Cooke, who resigned because of failing health.

Paying tribute to this 'de facto' Trustee and 'Elder Statesman' of the Association David Barham reminded listeners that Basil had been on the committee for 28 years, and had been honorary auditor since 1966.

The new 1985 season began with an unprecedented move, when Peter Clements issued a personal protest, allowed under RORC/IOR Rules, over the rating and age allowances allocated to the classic 'Sunstone'. It was a controversy which had festered on the circuit for several years, and Peter took his action with the full approval of the committee.

Everything was done in good part on both sides, and nobody had the slightest wish to question the integrity of Tom and Vicky Jackson, 'Sunstone's' very well liked owners.

The problem was that this 39ft 6ins classic wooden centre-board yacht, designed by the legendary American Olin Stephens, and launched on the Clyde in 1965, was just doing too well.

Her age allowances converted into a rating equivalent to a boat of 21ft 6ins. Ironically, the EAORA committee's own decision to apply a more generous age allowance than RORC Mark III(a) allowed to older boats was a contributing factor to the

Tom and Vicky Jackson - 1986

dispute. It was done in good faith in the hope of encouraging more owners of older boats to continue racing, but disgruntled owners of modern high-flyers could not believe that this could possibly be correct. When there was wind 'Sunstone' could out-reach modern three-quarter tonners, and when it fell light she could out-run them.

When the dispute became public knowledge it provoked comment and angry letters in the columns of the yachting press for months. What really got up everyone's nose was not just the fact that 'Sunstone' did so well when racing, but that she also enjoyed a dual role as a houseboat.

Tom and Vicky had always intended to live on a boat when they married in 1972, and in 1981 they bought 'Sunstone' because she was bigger than their previous home, supremely well built, and offered an after cabin. She was also about as big as the couple could handle on their own, and with a few very minor modifications she became their permanent home.

"Going racing was simply a matter of rolling up a strip of carpet and putting it ashore" they claimed, to the disbelieving astonishment of householders more burdened with domestic possessions who simply could not conceive of such a spartan existence.

The fashion for minimalist living, which would be perfectly well understood in the trendy 2000's was a long way in the future. People felt there must be a catch somewhere, when two people both with responsible jobs in higher education could apparently manage to live without visible possessions.

What everyone failed to take into account was the relationship forged by Tom and Vicky with every inch of their beloved boat. They knew exactly what she could do, and how far she could be pushed in any circumstances.

They also forgot the thousands of man and woman-hours, and every spare penny, poured into maintaining her honey-coloured varnish in the most immaculate condition. 'Sunstone's' repeated successes on the East Anglian circuit caused much muttering over the bars, and soured the air until Peter Clements went ahead with his appeal. It is a matter of record that 'Sunstone' was re-weighed and measured, and her rating and the appropriate age allowances were duly confirmed as correct.

Whether it was the protest, or simply the result of new jobs for both Tom and Vicky, the following season 'Sunstone' went to a new home at Brighton Marina, and later to the Hamble.

As a gesture of regret at their departure, and for all that had happened, the Association invited Tom and Vicky to be guests at the annual dinner in recognition of their contribution to the East Coast.

The pair continued to race in RORC events on the South Coast, where their skilful handling, and 'Sunstone's' remarkable abilities soon created similar tensions amongst the yacht-racing fraternity on the South Coast.

In 1985 they snatched the overall trophy in the RORC

Channel Race, against a field of Admiral's Cuppers, and followed it up by winning their class in the Fastnet.

Battle hardened works teams, particularly those coming from the States, were not remotely amused to find their victories looking somewhat hollow, while defeat by such an old yacht was acutely embarrassing.

Sigma 38 - 'Bullwinkle'

Still going strong in 1992, at the age of 27, 'Sunstone' was selected for the English team for the Rolex Commodore's Cup competition. Her remarkable record includes winning the IMS Points Championship in six out of seven years between 1989 and 1995. She was also named as the Silk Cut Yacht of the Year in 1986 and 1992.

At the time of writing 'Sunstone' had reached New Zealand in time for her owners to watch the finals of the 1999 America's Cup, and was halfway through a voyage round the world.

But the problem of classic boats with generous age allowances showed no sign of going away.

In 1985 Richard Matthews' four-year hold on the overall championship was broken by another classic. This was the 15 year old Sparkman & Stephens One Tonner 'Clarionet', now restored to immaculate condition by civil engineer John Breakell and his wife Linda of Haven Ports YC, who found her languishing on the

South Coast in 1985.

Affectionately known as 'The Log', 'Clarionet' was another 'Golden Oldie' who was always well sailed and proved unbeatable in most conditions. She would hold the championship twice more in 1986 and 1988. Another classic which regularly did well was Alan Major's S & S34 'Voile D'Or'.

Another S & S34 not seen since the 1970's also re-surfaced a year or so later in the shape of Dave Hunkins' beautifully restored 'Morning All'. She also proved very hard to beat, and won the Class III title in 1993.

The East Anglian Offshore Racing Association has always attracted a wide range of entrants and ambitions, despite all the controversies about allowances and measuring and however much it irritated the designers and owners of newer designs, there were plenty of people who could see little wrong with a system under which a well sailed and well maintained old boat could finish after 13 races and a lively season in all sorts of weather level-pegging for points with the latest SJ 35 Three-quarter tonner.

In Class III Chairman David Powell's 1978 designed Hustler 32 'Bright Spark' only narrowly beat the newest boat in the fleet - John Munn's Formula 28 'Impulsif' and rumoured to be capable of surfing down a wave at 15 knots!

As the committee juggled with statistics and theories there were plenty of optimists who pointed that enthusiasm was not declining, it was more a case of boats growing bigger, and demanding huge crews to man the weather rails who might previously have sailed 3 or 4 up in a larger fleet of smaller boats.

Nevertheless there were increasing calls for some 'humanization' of the annual programme; with later and more time-friendly starts. The old insistence on 50 miles as the minimum length for a race was also under fire, in favour of shorter but just as demanding courses with cross-tide legs, especially if this helped to avoid the dreaded 'tidal gate' which always afflicted one end of the fleet or the other.

More than anything competitors wanted some logic to the season's programme, that would not call for long delivery trips, or expensive berths in unfamiliar marinas.

By mid-way through the decade the hottest topic of discussion was the RORC's newly introduced Channel Handicap System, designed in co-operation with the French to provide a cheaper and more user-friendly rating system than the IOR. It was hoped the availability at low cost of a CHS certificate (£15) would encourage owners of older and less competitive boats to continue racing, while a system of self-measurement would do away with the need and expense of a visit from an official measurer.

The suggestion was first thrashed out by the committee in November 1984 and put to the Annual General Meeting, but failed to win agreement from competitors, who decided it would be preferable to tinker with the Age Allowance for older boats than to introduce a new and entirely separate division whose points would not be eligible for the season's overall trophies.

The subject was again raised at the 1985 annual meeting, by which time West Mersea YC who could claim some experience reported the new system to be 80 per cent successful, particularly with those yachts which had no hope of winning under IOR.

Despite continuing worries about some of the anomalies apparently being thrown up it was agreed to offer a trial CHS season, in a re-instated Class IV.

By the end of 1986 it was clear that the new division was working very successfully. Chairman David Powell reported that 35 yachts had raced under CHS without apparently affecting numbers in the three IOR classes, and entries had exceeded 20 for every race in the programme except the Sunk, then still being run as a night race.

He foresaw that the time would soon come when fleets were divided 50/50.

While the committee were reluctant to adopt CHS for all classes until they had a little more experience of the system, it was clear that Class IV had been popular and was likely to grow.

In the light of this they recommended scrapping the Association's enhanced old age allowance for 1987, and dropping Beta Division, since the needs of older boats were being met by CHS.

It was also agreed that CHS boats should be able to support their own clubs for the inter-club trophies, and it was agreed to score both divisions equally, and to take the best three results in each race regardless of system.

It was a season for small boats. In deciding where to award the Star Trophy Jim Humphris said if clubs were eligible rather than individuals, the trophy should go to the Medway YC.

The club's team of three Class III boats, 'Impulsif' (John Munns) 'Tom Bombadil' (Mike Chamberlain) and 'Misty' (Robin Prior) had travelled many miles to compete all round the region, two being powered only by outboard engines.

The Trophy was finally awarded to the quarter-tonner 'Tom Bombadil' who had competed in 14 races.

The winner of the CHS division was Des and Sue Cowan of Haven Ports YC with the Contessa 33 'Eclipse' in their first year of offshore racing.

Another threat facing the Association in 1987 was the RORC's proposal to drop the second East Coast Race, sailed from West Mersea to either Zeebrugge or Breskens, which would leave only the North Sea Race for anyone who wanted to qualify themselves or their crews for membership of the Fastnet Race.

East Anglian entries for the North Sea Race had already dropped badly, mainly because the dates planned to fit in with the

Dutch public holiday for Pentecost only occasionally co-incided with the British bank holiday weekend.

Owners were also concerned about the Category II requirement for RORC races, demanding more equipment than normally carried by EAORA yachts.

After negotiations the RORC agreed to organise a new 150 mile race from Burnham to Nieupoort in1988, in co-operation with the Royal Burnham YC which would be run under Category III and be part of the EAORA qualifying programme.

Quite understandably West Mersea were less than happy at losing their race, and in a Judgement of Solomon it was eventually agreed the RORC/EAORA race would alternate between West Mersea and the Royal Burnham. In West Mersea's year the race would replace their Sunk Race, an old established overnight fixture no longer attracting sufficient entries to survive.

East Anglian boats continued to do well in other spheres, John Breakell's 21 year old 'Clarionet' scoring an overall win in the RORC's 1987 Channel Race (which included top-notch competitors from around the world taking part in the Admiral's Cup) while Peter Dyer deprived himself of almost certain EAORA honours by taking the re-vamped 'Harmony 87' to the World Half Ton Cup.

The 1987 overall championship went to David Geaves' 'Fiona of Burnham' who also spent much of the season campaigning for the Three-quarter Ton Cup. 'The Red Dragon' now in the ownership of Patrick Lee took Class I and Richard Beale's 'Local Hero II' Class III, contributing to the Crouch Yacht Club's second successive victory in the Inter-Club competition.

Patrick's ambitious East Anglian Week in France had also proved a resounding success, and with the Crouch on such a roll, it seemed appropriate that he should also become the new chairman.

The Star Trophy was awarded to Roy Aspinall with 'Bellerophon of Mersea' in recognition of his stalwart support for the Association.

Aspinall would go on to become chairman of the Association from 1996-98 following the split from Sail East, but he would be the first to admit that by the late Eighties much of the spirit of EAORA as he had always experienced and enjoyed it, had begun to leach away.

"It all went wrong in the Eighties" he told me " It used to be a swashbuckling, hearty rugby-playing type of background - but everything had to change. Boats got bigger. Now to cheat the design rules you have to have a huge crew of 8 - 10 coolies sitting on the side with a choc bar." His was the philosophy of the early days.

As he recalls "I was just a little chap. The first time I did a Fastnet I was so proud to have a 24ft LWL boat and to be able to race offshore. We carried oil lights because we couldn't carry enough electricity to last the course. It was all great fun. That sort of thing doesn't exist any more."

The last three years had been ones of considerable change and upheaval, but with the change to CHS fully established Patrick soon set about putting his own inimitable style on things.

Out went committee meetings at the RORC in London. In came meetings at the Moat House Hotel at Harlow. The CHS division was split, divided by rating into light or heavy-weight classes.

Clubs were implored to ransack their trophy cupboards for cups which could be diverted to the new CHS divisions.

By the end of 1988 Patrick could report the most successful season for many years, with 80 boats racing. The Association seemed to be holding its own, despite a general falling in numbers over the whole yacht racing scene.

The Channel Handicap division also continued to thrive with support from over 50 yachts, ranging from a Swan 51 to Brian Tuckwood's Hunter Delta 26. "EAORA had once again become synonymous with good racing, good seamanship, good fellowship and good fun," he said.

This he attributed to a willingness to experiment with new ideas, such as the back-to-back weekends, and the new joint race from Burnham to Nieupoort with the RORC, which he pointed out had attracted 38 entries.

A number of competitors had thus been lured into doing their first RORC race, which promised well for the future.

Channel Handicap having proved itself, the 1988 AGM agreed to retain an IOR element in a new Alpha division for those boats, notably the three-quarter tonners which did not rate well under the new system.

While the move to Channel Handicap was almost inevitable, it created almost as many administrative problems as it solved. Safety regulations had to be re-written, the donors of old trophies persuaded to allow them to be re-allocated, anomalies ironed out to enable yachts who wished to qualify for the Royal Thames Championship to race in either division.

In the wider world, it was also becoming increasingly obvious that CHS as a system was inadequate to cope with the wilder fringes of design.

The IOR system had been scrapped, accused of producing unseaworthy monstrosities, in which stability was sacrificed for speed, structural integrity for lightweather performance, and seakindliness for rating gain, but it seemed the new one was no better.

CHS was always slightly suspect, because of the self-measurement aspect, which could lead to anomalies, and the secrecy which surrounded the computation of ratings. Despite this supposed secrecy, designers were soon pushing at the limits. The result was a new breed of ever smaller stripped out racing machines, overgrown dinghies whose rudimentary accommodation could not stand comparision with the more cruiser-orientated competitors on the circuit.

Clearly, in the long run, some kind of two-tier system which would separate high-technology and the state of the art designs from the more conventional cruiser/racer was needed.

Almost as soon as CHS had established itself there were rumours of yet another handicapping system, as in IMS, which instead of measuring boats against their opposition, rated them against a theoretical best performance in given conditions.

As we all now recognise IMS never caught on, except in semi-professional circles, and has since been superseded by yet another system, but the years of confusion between all the new initiatives must surely carry a share of the blame for much of the decline in enthusiasm for offshore sailing.

It was particularly resented at grass-roots level that anyone who resisted IMS for the perfectly valid reason that it was totally unsuitable to their traditional type of coastal racing was made to feel like a recalcitrant dinosaur.

John Breakell's 'Clarionet' with 'Speakeasy'

This attitude certainly contributed to the demise of East Anglian support for the North Sea Race, which was dominated by IMS rated Dutch entries, while the English CHS rated boats were treated as second class citizens by the national authority.

At the same time there was cause for optimism with new concepts, and design ideas coming on stream: RORC support for a new one-design light displacement production yacht spawned several contenders, amongst them the Sigma 38 and the Lightwave 395, built at Oyster Marine.

Amongst East Anglians who went for the Lightwave were David Powell with 'Concept' and Peter Clements with 'Carronade'.

The Oswald twins, John and Ric equipped themselves with the twin Sigma 38's 'Sidewinder' and 'Dabula Manzi' while Peter and Katie Whiteley's 'Bullwinkle' was the third boat to represent the RBYC.

At the other end of the spectrum amongst the small boats in Class III, we have already seen John Mullins' Formula 28 'Impulsif'. The 1988 season saw the first appearance of Robbie Stewart's Rob Humphreys MG30 half-tonner 'Secrets', which was reported to have clocked

'Carronade'

15.7 knots as she surfed down the Wallet to become a runaway winner of the Sunk Race.

In a notably tough season 'Secrets' was runner up to 'Fiona of Burnham' for the overall IOR championship, while the CHS Division went to 'Clarionet'.

By 1989, and the Association's 40th season, the move to CHS was complete, and with everyone united under one handicapping system, entries were the best for a decade.

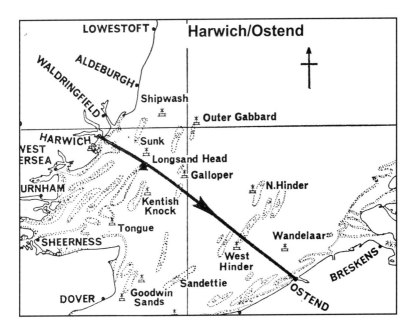

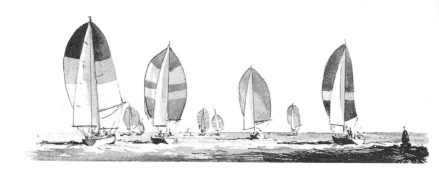

CHAPTER SEVEN

RACE - WEEKS

"A lot of people enjoyed themselves immensely, which is hopefully what it is all about" 'Yachts & Yachting 1981'

THE FIRST East Anglian Race Week was held in 1981, setting a style which, over the next two decades would make the event one of the most popular in the season's programmes.

The Week itself seems to be a concept unique to the East Coast, of which the Association should be extremely proud.

I do not know of any other organisation which supports a week of sailing and socializing, usually in a foreign venue, during which skippers and crews live aboard, travel from port to port, and use their boats as most were originally intended, as cruiser/racers.

The Week becomes a rumbustious caravanserai of fellow-travellers, with a common purpose to enjoy some hard competitive sailing, and some equally hard partying. It matters not whether the boat is a Class I hot-shot, a family-crewed 26 footer dipping the first toe into the racing scene, or a motor cruiser requisitioned to act as a mother ship to a stripped out racing machine.

All are welcome, and all enjoy themselves, even,

surprisingly, our hosts in foreign parts who seem to view the invasion of partying hordes with complete equanimity.

As we have seen earlier, East Anglian sailors have had a long tradition of supporting the Flevo Week series in Holland. In 1969, David Cole of the Medway, an overall winner of the series with 'Brigand Chief' suggested to the AGM that the Association should organise a similar event.

The idea was enthusiastically supported by Basil Chichester-Cooke, who suggested it should be called "the Cabbage Patch series" (a reference to the then popular American "Onion Patch" series). But nothing could be done at the time. The annual programme was already overcrowded, and chairman Jack Williams had to admit that the level of support and administrative skills around the member clubs who would be involved was not up to the task.

The idea did not come to fruition for nearly a decade, by which time the Level Rating competitions were losing impetus, entries in general were falling off, and every organisation was seeking a solution. Ian Marks of Blackwater SC revived the idea in 1979 hoping the cruising-in-company aspect of the series would encourage the more traditionally minded owners, while also bringing in some newcomers.

The first Race Week was incorporated into the 1981 season, with Haven Ports YC and Suffolk Yacht Harbour at Levington as the focal point.

I cannot trace who was the Race Officer in charge, but the committee boat was George Farmer's fine sea-going 'Olivebank'

By current standards the Week was nothing if not ambitious. Just to read the programme induces exhaustion, especially as there were no discards. Festivities started with a dinner at West Mersea on the Friday night to precede the Crouch YC's Houghton Cup 64-mile course from Mersea to Burnham. That night, for the first time, the Club entertained an East Anglian fleet providing dinner and a steel band. Day Two saw a short 30-mile non-qualifying feeder race back through the Spitway in time for dinner at West Mersea.

Day Three began with a late afternoon start for the 60-mile overnight Sunk Race, finishing at Harwich with a lay-day at Suffolk Yacht Harbour, and a dinner in the evening. On Wednesday the Royal Harwich YC's 65-mile Shipwash Race was followed by a buffet supper at Haven Ports YC.

Thursday offered a little light exercise with a 15 mile pursuit race on an Olympic or Haven Series type course around Dovercourt Bay, to raise money for the RNLI. At 4.00pm the same day the fleet set off on the Walton Trophy, a 65-mile night race from Harwich to Lowestoft, over the traditional course around the Shipwash and Outer Gabbard light-ships.

Friday was a much-needed lay-day, followed by a formal dinner at the Royal Norfolk & Suffolk YC, after which, at 6.00am the following morning the fleet set off for the 45-mile Lowestoft-Harwich race, finishing up with a prize-giving and end-of-week party hosted by the Royal Harwich YC.

The major prize for the week was the County Standard Trophy donated by Colchester based Essex County Newspapers, whose chairman was the notable East Coast maritime historian and writer Hervey Benham.

Ian Marks (whose confectionery manufacturing company Trebor Ltd also put up £500 to sponsor the Week) presented a handsome silver Cigarette Box for Class I; Brian Foulger presented the 'Ailish Cup' for Class II and Mike Spear provided a trophy for Class III (currently known as the Secretary's Plate, but records do not indicate if this is the original trophy.)

Looking back with hindsight, it seems astonishing that this arduous programme did not appear to discourage anybody.

The Week was voted to have been a great success, very

largely due to the good weather which prevailed. Seventy-five boats took part, making a total of 290 starts in the seven races, of which two short inshores did not count for points.The most successful, and winner of the County Standard Trophy was the three-quarter-tonner Dehler DB1 'Senta of Mersea' owned by Doctors A. Antcliff and G. Rankin, and skippered for the series by the East Coast sailmaker Mike Richardson. The runner-up was Ron Wigley's 'Wizard' another West Mersea boat, and third place went to 'Barna Pearl' owned by Archie Clark, Commodore of the Royal Cinque Ports YC.

The fleet also included 'Nadia' built by Richard Matthews, as a contender for the Admiral's Cup, which had sailed non-stop from St Malo in order to take part. Matthews was rewarded for his efforts with a win in the Sunk Race, his second in the EAORA season, which was to help bring him the first of his five subsequent East Anglian championships.

The closest competition throughout the week was between the six Hustler 32's, who included Frank Reed's 'Tramp'; Ron Wigley's 'Wizard'; Harry Croker's 'Cheetah'; Len Jones' 'Hesitation Roll'; Dr Ann Rodway's 'Witch Doctor' and David Cassidy's 'Fiddler'. Entries for the Week read like a roll-call of almost all the major competitors at this period, and included: Ian Marks ('Peppermint'); John Wiltshier ('The Red Dragon', designed by Andrew Stewart); Terry Swann (Hustler, 'Bright Spark') Alan Major (S & S34 'Voile D'Or') Mike Spear ('Moon Boots'); Richard Oxley ('Red Shamrock'); Danny Donoghue ('Shazoom'); Harry Tribe (1967 Kim Holman designed 'Lynx'); Terry Vernon ('Magical Mr Mistoffelees', the prototype Hustler 27); David Cole (GK34 'Patanda'); Peter Clements ('Carronade'); Mike Evers ('Espada'); Kit Hobday (GK34 'Geriatric Bear') and Anna and Chris Brooke ('Paladin').

Despite the number of sea-miles, competitors still had

plenty of stamina for the social side, including a memorable lunch party at Rodney Hill's home in West Mersea, hosted by his wife Jill the current EAORA secretary.

Members of Haven Ports YC, one of the newest clubs in the Association, turned cooks and caterers to put on another magnificent occasion in a marquee pitched alongside their ex-Trinity house lightship clubhouse in Suffolk Yacht Harbour.

It is recalled that the party went on into the small hours, regardless (or oblivious!) of the low spring tides, which meant everyone had to be up at 4.00am the next morning to be sure of getting out in time to make their next start.

The whole event created a lot of interest in the yachting press, much of it from the pen of John Harrison, for many years a correspondent for 'Yachts & Yachting' and a variety of newspapers.

'Yachts & Yachting' gave the Week two full pages of pre-view, followed by almost the same space for a report of the week, commenting "Anyone who was around the scene, or more especially took part, will know that an awful lot of people enjoyed themselves immensely, which is hopefully what it is all about." In conclusion he added "The atmosphere was terrific and must have been rewarding to the EAORA committee which had felt it was sticking its neck out in introducing such an ambitious programme. No doubt there will be some criticism, but on the whole this new format for a passage racing circus seems to have gone like the proverbial bomb...."

At their de-briefing meeting the committee privately agreed that the programme had been perhaps a bit too arduous and should not have included two night races. It also felt the Week should stand alone as a series, with races tailored to fit, rather than attempting to include elements from the traditional programme which might then be sailed in alternate years. The main concern was whether the Week should be an annual event or held in alternate seasons as an attraction in non-Fastnet years. If this was so they were already committed to a second Week in 1982, and Len Baldwin from the Medway YC was appointed to organise it.

This was held earlier in the season, and centred further south, starting with a reception at the Royal Corinthian YC before the Thames Estuary race to the Medway.

The points races included the Thames Estuary and the Jane's Cup, plus the Royal Temple YC's Beadles Challenge Cup for a race to Ostend, and the Royal Harwich YC's race back to Harwich.

The programme also included two days of round-the-cans racing from Ramsgate and Ostend. The overall winner was Kit Hobday with 'Geriatric Bear'.

Once again host clubs were responsible for the starts and finishes. In addition they were issued with copious lists of food and drink to be placed aboard the committee boat 'Olivebank' at every stop!

No other records seem to exist for this second week, but it was clearly a success and set a pattern for the future.

From the post-week questionnaire it was also clear that competitors had little enthusiasm for visiting East Coast ports, and would much prefer to go foreign.

Coming down firmly in favour of a biennial (and to be largely financially self-supporting) event the committee appointed David Powell to organise the 1984 week. George Farmer's 'Olivebank' was once again the committee boat, with Paul Edden of Haven Ports as race officer.

Strenuous efforts were made by Jim McNaughten of West Mersea and others to involve the Dutch and other foreign competition and to revive the old Cannon Ball trophy, but although agreement was reached in principle with the Royal Netherlands

YC no Dutch boats could be found to take part.

Action started with West Mersea's Sunk Race to Ramsgate, and the Royal Temple's Beadales Cup took the fleet to Ostend the following day, with a layday to follow in which to enjoy the hospitality of the North Sea YC.

On Tuesday the return race was an 80-miler back to Harwich, where the fleet would be based for the next three nights at Suffolk Yacht Harbour.

The author, who became secretary of the Association in succession to Jill Hill in November 1982 was aboard 'Olivebank' and remembers the night race as one of the most magical crossings of the North Sea one could imagine.

"It was a clear night, with amazing visibility, and half-way over one could pick up the loom of the lights from both sides. As we passed through the fleet they were all on the same fetch, and as they dropped away behind us their port hand lights were strung out across the horizon like a perfect ruby necklace.

"It was a very fast race, but George was always reluctant to use full power, and we only just made it into Dovercourt Bay and slung an anchor on the finishing line before 'Sidewinder' John Oswald's new One Tonner designed by Hugh Welbourne came powering over the horizon."

The overall trophy for the week was won for the second year by Kit Hobday, this time with the new 'Erotic Bear' who excused herself from the final night race back to Burnham on the grounds that she had already amassed enough points to win the week, a decision which did not endear him to the rest of the fleet.

This race, recalls the present chairman (Stephen Gosling 1999-2001) included a dead beat through the Swin Spitway in the early hours of Saturday morning!

The fourth week was held in 1986, when the overall winner was Peter Clements with 'Carronade V' and to open up the competition for those whose boats stayed to do the whole week (rather than just those races which qualified for the season) the Crouch YC presented the Mary Hill Trophy for a mid-week series.

The only incident to mar the Week was a dispute over the final race from Ostend. The North Sea YC having inadvertently double-booked the harbour the EAORA sailing committee decided to solve the problem by starting the race home a little earlier in the day, using an ad hoc line between the Casino and a small buoy off the beach.

Despite strenuous efforts to alert every competitor, they failed to find 'Sage', a newcomer to the fleet, which had not competed mid-week, and did not appear to still be in Ostend. By the time Owen Croft arrived on the ferry to compete in the race he had very little time to make the earlier start-time, and duly protested to the race committee.

The protest by 'Sage' resulted in redress of average points, which made no difference to the week's major results, but it was a salutory warning to race committee's not to tamper with the published Sailing Instructions, even with the best of intentions!

The decision to use the Casino line almost provoked an international incident. While 'Olivebank' hovered in the harbour to take off the race committee, Jim McNaughten and his team were driven along the Promenade to do their stuff. But at the sound of the first gun the Belgian authorities woke up and hastily mobilized their forces to find out what was going on. Shot-guns it appeared, were definitely out of order on the Promenade, and the team just had time to complete the starting sequence, before beating a rapid retreat, leaping aboard 'Olivebank' just in time to avoid arrest.

By 1987 competitors were becoming bored with the North Sea ports and were ready for something more ambitious. There was a Gallic glint in Patrick Lee's eye after the ever-enthusiastic Irishman from the Crouch YC had carried out a detailed reconnaissance of the delights of the French coast. He convinced the committee that Fecamp was the place to go. Despite some resistance from those who felt it difficult to justify counting the Channel within the normal boundaries of East Anglia, all doubts were carried away by Patrick's infectious enthusiasm, and with total disregard of any logistical problems the die was cast for France.

The problems were not long in coming. 'Olivebank' being unavailable, the choice of committee boat fell on an elderly motor-yacht 'Iraine' owned by Harry and Renee Chandler from Burnham, a wonderfully colourful couple, who were founders of the Upminster Travel Club and one of the earliest agents to bring foreign holidays within reach of the common man.

The offer was generous but it would have been hard to find any boat less like the stable, sea-kindly 'Olivebank' or one less well prepared for her role, not having any equipment aboard, or the benefit of a haul-out and scrub for many months.

Bob Stewart of Royal Burnham skippered 'Iraine' while Peter Clements, winner of the previous year's Week offered to find out what life was like on the other side of the fence, by acting as race officer, assisted by John Greenhalgh from the 'Carronade' crew.

The Channel itself threw up a few unexpected problems, such as the buoys which had been chosen as being geographically well-placed for start or finish lines, with casual unconcern over the depth of water to be encountered when attempting to anchor in the vicinity.

The sailing committee aboard 'Iraine' was eternally grateful to Danny Donoghue of the Crouch YC who was following the fleet with 'Malouine' a heavy displacement yacht which being properly equipped with a suitable length of anchor chain, was pressed into service as an auxiliary committee boat when required.

Patrick's determination to find a sponsor, and to extend East Anglian hospitality to a yacht crewed by a majority of disabled sailors, created quite another complication. It was a Quixotic gesture (and much appreciated by those taking part) but sadly the deficiencies in the boat provided made it quite unsuitable for such a crew racing in such a competitive fleet.

However hard they tried (and they certainly did that) the unfortunate crew were doomed to be tail-end-Charlie in every race, forcing the race officer who had to get the fleet back into port in time for the evening events, into an unenviable choice between shortening course unnecessarily early, or pulling the plug on the disabled boat.

To make up for their disappointments on the water the disabled crew turned out to be determined party animals, almost invariably the last to leave the clubhouse every night, usually by way of a wheel-chair race down the pontoon.

The first stop was Boulogne, and on Sunday morning the fleet set off for the 80 mile passage to Fecamp. But the wind failed to oblige, and what should have been a pleasant sail turned into a 24 hour marathon for those who had chosen the inshore option.

Some crews, who had started their holiday with a delivery trip from Harwich and had been unable to pick up more supplies found themselves distinctly short of food and water.

Among them the crew of Richard Beales half-tonner 'Local Hero II' from the Crouch were forced to exist on one bottle of water and a couple of stale baguettes throughout the long hot day, and were ready to eat the floorboards by the time they reached Fecamp.

Once installed in the French port the fleet received a tremendous welcome from the local yacht club (and from the harbourmaster who, as it subsequently appeared, had only half-believed in Patrick's expansive promises to produce such a large fleet!). Parties were laid on, and special marks set offshore for two short triangle day races.

The fun was over all too soon, and on Thursday the fleet raced back to Boulogne, followed by a short hop to Ramsgate for the new Terry Swann Salver, and a prizegiving party at the Royal Temple YC.

The overall winner of the week was Mike Harrison of the Crouch YC with 'Jiminy Cricket'.

Despite all difficulties, the 1987 Week turned out to be a great success, and the choice of the Channel ports as a venue raised the whole event into a new dimension.

Patrick Lee stepped into the chair of the Association in 1987, in succession to David Powell. He now had the bit firmly between the teeth, planning to take East Anglian Week to yet another new destination in 1988 and to involve more family-crews by setting the mid-week series in the more relaxed and sheltered inland waters of Holland.

In deference to the keen racing types, who were inclined to see Patrick's plans as a dumbing-down of the whole event, there were still to be three serious qualifying races for the season's points trophies.

Following an 84-mile downhill sleigh-ride from Harwich to Zeebrugge those seeking points did a short passage race on the following day to enter the Ooster Schelde through the forbidding-looking Roompot Sluis, while other boats travelled to Flushing and up through the canals via the fleshpots of Middleburg and Veere.

Patrick had chosen the lovely old town of Zierikzee as the base for the next two days, where crews made serious inroads into the local moules mariniere, the Grolsch beer and the Genever (both oude and jong) while waiting for everyone to re-assemble.

By day race officer Peter Duce of the Crouch YC set

The daily briefing for Race officer Paul Edden 1984

testing inshore races around the cans in the Roompot, and the weather deteriorated until the final event of the short series took place in such blinding rain that it was virtually impossible to see one end of the line from the other.

When the mid-week party was washed-out only Patrick's Irish genius could have thought of chartering the local ferry-boat for an

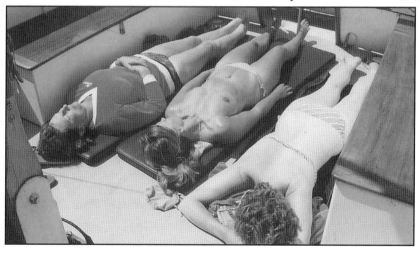

It's not all hard work on the committee boat! 'Olivebank' 1984

141

impromptu party - and of persuading the astonished Captain that it was all good fun!

As the gale continued there was no option but to cancel the race home to Harwich, after the Dutch authorities flatly refused to allow the fleet to lock out through the Roompot Sluis, and the Week ended in some disarray as skippers made a dash for home through the canals, while others abandoned their boats and went home by ferry.

At Haven Ports YC where John Margetson had organised a prize-giving dinner there were 160 un-eaten meals to dispose of, and it was as a direct result of this fiasco that all subsequent Weeks have finished with a party on foreign shores.

At this stage the East Anglian fleet was in transition between two rating rules, with 11 still racing under IOR and 28 under the new Channel Handicap. It is also notable that the entries came from 13 of the Association's member clubs.

The IOR division went to C.J. Robinson's 'Fever' who won both offshore races, despite losing her Windex while negotiating the entrance to the Roompot Sluis.

John and Linda Breakell's veteran classic 'Clarionet' took the CHS division. The short series was won by the Galloper Syndicate from the Royal Temple YC with the SJ35 'Intention'.

By 1989 Patrick was ready for another adventure trail, this time an even more ambitious programme which would take the fleet as far down-channel as Deauville. It

Cartoonist in the crew

142

was a huge undertaking, not least in view of the disparity in size between the fleet of more than 40 boats, which ranged from a 45ft Barracuda to a 27ft Hunter Delta, with somewhere around 300 competitors. This was the hey-day of the new breed of fast light-displacement boats such as the Sigma 38, the Lightwave 395's.

A huge entry in Class I included John Oswald's Sigma 38 'Sidewinder' plus four other Sigma 38's, three Lightwaves, and John Breakell's elegant classic Swan 44 'Born Free' which had replaced 'Clarionet'.

The Week was in trouble almost before it began, when a last minute refusal by the French authorities to accept the fleet in Boulogne because of

George Farmer preparing to fire the winning gun for 'The Red Dragon' 1986

on-going repair work to the harbour pontoons meant the first race would have to go direct from Ramsgate to Fecamp, a distance of 120 miles.

With the wind and tide building against them off Dover, several boats decided to take the inshore option down the English coast, only to find themselves between the devil and the deep as they tried to cross the entrance while irate ferries approaching from all directions started to radio the port authorities.

Other boats made straight for the French coast and ducked

into Boulogne feeling that whatever problems the French had could not be worse than another 80 miles at sea.

As the Dover authorities became increasingly apoplectic at this invasion of their space the race committee aboard Chris Petrie's 'Lady Coppelia' being unable to communicate with their errant fleet, could only keep silence and hope for the best.

Eventually the front went through, the wind eased, and by morning the scattered fleet was beginning to re-assemble, having made good progress to Fecamp. Amongst those awaiting the tail-enders at Fecamp were Peter Jackson of the Royal Temple YC and the crew of 'Oblivion Express'.

'Oblivion' had lost the top section of her mast in the heavy seas off Dover, but true to the East Anglian spirit the crew had motored back to Ramsgate, enjoyed a couple of games of snooker before catching the ferry to France and had driven the 80 miles to Fecamp where they bedded down for the remainder of the night in the yacht club! The rest of the week enjoyed glorious weather, and

A committee boat start from 'Iraine' off Fecamp 1987

First football match - Deauville 1989

when the fleet was finally safely locked into the harbour at Deauville, Peter Clements came up with the idea of whiling away the afternoon with a football match on the beach.

While the wives and daughters went window-shopping around the luxury establishments of this elegant French watering-hole, fifty-a-side teams, drawn from Burnham and West Mersea versus The Rest of the World brawled like Mad Dogs and Englishmen in the sand, watched by a bewildered

Fashion Parade - Deauville 1989

145

French audience.

The football match was to become a cherished tradition of all future EAORA weeks and has since been played on all manner of pitches in France and Holland.

The 1990 Race Week returned to Holland when more than 50 yachts signed on for the first weekend, which included two qualifying races, from Harwich-Ostend, and Ostend-Breskens.

It was a fast passage, with Richard Matthews breaking all previous records with a time of 8hrs 13mins to Ostend in his converted ex-12 metre 'Crusader'. Strong winds continued the next day for a fast and bumpy ride to Breskens, before the fleet dived into the canal system at Flushing for a leisurely lay day passage to Kortgene. The mid-week series was sailed in the Ousterschelde with a two-night stop-over at the quaint and historic town of Goes, where the harbour master had cleared the whole of

Waiting for the wind in Holland 1990. Left to right - Rosemary Beeson (Timekeeper) Jo Barker and Peter Duce (Race officers)

Battleflag flying 'Axeman' (Ron Lewis CYC) leads the charge through the canals from Flushing to Middleburg, 1990

the inner harbour for a wall-to-wall raft-up of British boats.

One never ceases to be astonished at the warmth of the welcome accorded to EAORA fleets around a variety of Dutch ports in successive years, despite the sometimes rowdy parties and water-fights which ensued. Indeed Goes rapidly became one of the fleet's favourite watering-holes, to be revisited many times in the next few years.

The Week was notable for excellent racing, with just four points separating Robbie Stewart's 'Blush' and David and Annie Chatterton's 'Sensor' on the final race. This time, after being runner-up for the Week's honours twice, it was the Chatterton's year and they collected trophies for both long and short series, as well as the two Sigma 38 trophies.

An equally popular winner in Class II with 'The Red Dragon' was Patrick Lee, who after doing so much to promote the Race Weeks, was in his last year as chairman of the Association.

Busy start line in Holland - 1991

Close quarters with a Dutch Botter!

Class III went to Nigel Theadom with the Stephen Jones 17 year old and famously successful quarter-tonner 'Odd Job'.

The sight of the lanky red-headed rigger, crammed in some out-elbows fashion into this tiny, but intensely competitive boat, is one of the Week's most vivid memories, especially for the chasing-pack in his class.

Patrick Lee was succeeded as chairman by Peter Clements, another stalwart supporter of the Week, who decided that the 9th EAORA Week in 1991 should visit a new area of Holland. Reconnoitred and organised by Chris Goldsmith and John Margetson of Haven Ports YC, the opening race from Harwich to Zeebrugge was followed by a passage race north to enter the inland waterways through the Hellevoetsluis.

Of the 50 boats which completed the first weekend, more than 40 remained for a mid-week series of passage races, with a number of new stop-overs as they threaded their way through the waterways from the Hollandsch Diep via the Volkerak and back into the Ousterschelde. One of the most popular stop-overs, though possibly not with our long-suffering hosts, was Willemstadt, with its ancient seven-sided castle built by William of Orange in 1583.

It was another week of notably good racing, especially in Class II where 16 entries included three hotly competitive DB1's sailed by Peter Jackson and Paul Pearson from the Royal Temple. and Drs Webb and O'Riordan from the Medway. Once again Nigel Theadom and 'Odd Job' dominated Class III, taking both the week's trophies after some epic battles with Peter Dyer of the Crouch with 'Harmony '87'. One feature of this EAORA week was an attempt to revive Anglo-Dutch competition, by joining forces with the Dutch for one day of their Delta Week regatta.

There was plenty of goodwill on both sides, and the Dutch authorities went to immense lengths to convert the English CHS ratings into a viable NKK figure, but with the majority of the serious Dutch players away on their long offshore race, the racing was a bit one-sided.

Nevertheless a good day was had by all, and few will forget the awe-inspiring spectacle of 24 traditional Dutch botters, carrying a full complement of sail in their designated race, as they charged through the starting line for the combined NKK fleet totally oblivious of any polite niceties such as trying to keep clear of the line.

As Peter Clements remarked with admirable tolerance in his prizegiving speech - "A botter will go where a botter will go, and there's not much you can do except keep out of its way."

Despite dire predictions that few of the smaller competitors would be persuaded to face a 128-mile crossing of the North Sea, the 1992 Race Week headed for Northern Holland and the waters of the Ijselmeer. The crossing to Ijmuiden was not a problem for regular crews, but was a big step for smaller or less experienced competitors, and the organisers were delighted when no fewer than 19 Class III boats signed up for the trip out of a fleet of 36.

In one of the windiest seasons on record the first race turned into a white-knuckle sleigh-ride which had crews gasping on the edge between control and total wipe-out. Robbie Stewart's 'Blush' designed as a conversion of the Lightwave 395 by his brother Andrew, and which was at her best in heavy weather made the crossing from Harwich in just four minutes over 14 hours, clocking a top speed of 19.7 knots.

Luckily apart from shredded spinnakers and some gear damage the rest of the fleet arrived without mishap, and having caught their breath, set off into the North Sea Canal for the passage to Muiden.

The passage was hardly less dramatic than the race across, as yachts motored amongst large sea-going ships through torrential rain and thunderstorms during which at least two boats were struck

Victorious crew of 'Sensor' in Dutch Race Week 1990

by lightning, knocking out their electrics.

The Royal Netherlands YC welcomed the fleet warmly to their headquarters at Muiden while they picked up the pieces, after which they plunged off into the great inland sea of the Isjelmeer for passage races to the historic ports of Enkhuisen, Hoorn and Medemblik.

Despite the weather which barely relented all week, racing was extremely lively as some of the bigger boats found to their cost when trying to come to terms with the unusual steering effects created by racing while also ploughing a furrow in the mud.

It was a wonderful week for competition with the Chatterton's new Sigma 400 'Sensor' barely out of her wrapping paper; while at the other end of the spectrum Mr & Mrs Dave Hunkin from Haven Ports were sweeping the board with their 20

Relaxing after the race, Enkhuisen

Barbecuing at Enkhuisen for the Class I Party

year old and now beautifully restored S & S34 'Morning All' which attracted many a nostalgic eye.

As always apres-sail played a big part in the Week, with the nearest thing ever to an international incident occurring in Enkhuisen when the harbour-master took deep exception to a huge barbecue burning fiercely on the after-deck of Patrick Lee's 'The Red Dragon' during the Class I party.

The now traditional football match was played on

the hallowed turf of the Medemblik Football Club, but the 30-a-side teams (shirtless if you lived south of West Mersea) seemed unlikely to feature in any professional league.

Peter Clements' final flourish as Chairman was a return visit to France in 1993. It was the most ambitious Week yet, with those competitors who had to deliver to Dover beforehand covering more than 1000 miles.

The first race took the fleet to the newly opened Sovereign Harbour at Eastbourne. This was followed by a cross-channel leg to Le Havre, where the fleet were generously hosted by the Society des Regates de Le Havre for a mid-week series of day races in Seine bay, with overnight stops at Fecamp, Honfleur and Ouistreham, where we joined in the celebrations for Bastille Day.

It was nobody's fault that this ambitious programme co-

Chris Brooke, Brian Foulger on the committee boat 'Errona' France 1993

Peter Clements and Nigel Theadom sharing the Mary Hill trophy in Le Havre 1993

incided with a prolonged period of stormy weather, when for days on end it blew hard and steadily from the south-west, with torrential rain-storms to mar the well-earned lay-day in Honfleur.

Everyone had their problems, not least race officers Chris and Anna Brooke of Walton & Frinton YC in 'Errona' who managed to organise good racing in atrocious conditions, while also making impossible judgements about when to call a halt, so that boats could reach the next port in time to lock in.

The two hot-shots of the week were the Sigma 400's 'Independent Bear' (Kit Hobday) and 'Sensor' (David & Annie Chatterton) while Nigel Theadom's newly acquired Toledo 30 'Djinn Seng' took Class III and missed out on the week's overall prize by only the smallest margin from the 'Bear'.

There was a notable turn-out of three-quarter tonners from the Royal Temple YC's fleet for the opening race, of which five including 'Street Legal (Guy Oury) and 'Second Luv' (Paul Smith) remained for the week to do battle with Peter and Katie Whiteley's much-travelled Sigma 38 'Bullwinkle'.

Thanks to determined efforts by a few stalwart supporters such as Stephen Gosling (Chairman 1990-2001). East Anglian weeks have continued, albeit on a smaller scale throughout the late Nineties.

They have been much enjoyed by those who have taken part, although the numbers have never approached those of the earlier years which made them such a special experience.

It is all part of the general demise of offshore racing, the increasing pressure on people's financial and social lives, and the design of modern boats which is hardly conducive to comfortable living or cruising.

Nevertheless it is claimed by those who have taken part recently that the very exclusiveness of a small fleet has allowed them to visit many of the smaller ports in Holland which would have been unable to accommodate 30-40 boats.

Prizegiving at the 'Societe des Regates' 1993

155

It has also increased the cameraderie between competitors, enabling crews from all sizes of boat to get together.

In 2001 when the Week is once again going to the Ousterschelde great efforts are being made to involve the Dutch, with plans to revive a team race between the two countries for the long neglected Cannon Ball Trophy, and to race once again in company with the Delta Fleet.

Race Week 1999

CHAPTER EIGHT

THE NINETIES:
and on to a Half-Century

AT THE beginning of the Nineties, competitors from the East Coast made their mark in a variety of more far-reaching events.

In 1990 the heavily hyped Brent Walker European Cup Race to Spain, attracted no fewer than six EAORA yachts.

Starters from Brighton Marina included Peter and Katie Whiteley's Sigma 38 'Bullwinkle'; James Mattison's Carter Three-quarter tonner 'Prairie Oyster' and John Oswald's chartered Maxi 'Surveyor' all from the RBYC; 'Bellerophon of Mersea' (Capt Roy Aspinall) from West Mersea, and 'Moustique' (Mike Spear) from Haven Ports.

In 1990 the Star Trophy went to Doug Ellis of Haven Ports for his efforts in 'Rainbow' in the Yachting Monthly Triangle Race. And in 1992 the eyes of the sailing world focussed on Mike Taylor Jones and his son Will from Royal Harwich as they battled their way in the 20 year old S & S 'Deerstalker' in the Teeside Round Britain Race.

'Deerstalker' originally built in 1973 for Joe Isaacs of Walton & Frinton YC was the smallest boat in the race, and by the final leg she only had to save her time on Chris Little's 45.5 Beneteau 'Bounder' over the last 360 miles from Hartlepool to Cowes to take the top place.

Their chances seemed to have gone as they battled gales in the North Sea, and tidal gates in the Channel but the gallant little 'Deerstalker' and her crew held her own through everything the elements could throw at them to snatch the trophy.

Another East Anglian entrant who figured in the same event was the veteran 'Brandy Bottle' jointly owned by Roger Utting and Rudi Polednik of Haven Ports. They were awarded the Association's Star Trophy for their efforts.

It is always difficult to write about personalities who are still active in the present time, but at this point in the account of

Living up to her name 'Carronade' prepares to fire a broadside as she passes under Tower Bridge in the RORC's Millennium Sail Past

the Association's history it is perhaps the moment to salute some who have put their names on EAORA trophies, without receiving adequate mention in earlier chapters.

Amongst them is Peter Clements (Chairman 1990-93) who has given unstinting support with a succession of 'Carronades' not to mention numerous stints on the committee, and much burning of the midnight oil grappling with the finer details of ratings, points and the Cox Sprague System. Unlike most sailors he has also seen life on the other side of the starting line, as race officer for EAORA week, and can also be held responsible for the introduction of the EAORA Week football match, and many memorable parties.

Peter's one-time part-owner Harvey Spero also deserves a specially grateful mention from the author (EAORA Secretary 1982-94) as the only person who could get us out of a hole in Holland by picking up the tab for an entire Race Week Prizegiving Party on his 'Gold card' without batting an eyelid.

Race Weeks would not be complete either without David and Annie Chatterton and their long-term crew Tony and Chuffy Merewether whom I believe have never missed a RaceWeek with a succession of 'Sensor's.

Nor would West Mersea's contribution be complete without mention of Frank Reed, who after a long career with 'Tramp' is now more usually encountered as principal race officer for the RORC's most prestigious events. Frank has been a tower of strength, never failing to offer wise advice, or to keep the Association on track over the preparation of Sailing Instructions, and all race management matters, for which as EAORA Secretary I have much cause for gratitude.

With an EAORA record of thirteen Class Trophies & five overall championships David Geaves of Royal Burnham has a record unlikely ever to be beaten.

He has supported EAORA for over 30 years, and figured briefly in an earlier chapter with 'St George' and 'Corrie'.

'St George' was built at Brooke Marine for Roger De Quincey, a founder member of the Association. She was intended to be the first of a One Design class of similar style to the International Dragon, but the resulting craft bore little relationship to any accepted rule and was always hugely handicapped. She was nick-named 'The Flying Breadknife'.

David remembers "She was 20ft on the waterline. She had an International 14 mast, one set of shrouds and about four spreaders. Things used to break. She was not wet by the standards of heavy displacement boats of that time. She was beautifully built, and very buoyant."

One feels that this remarkable craft must have caused much the same consternation amongst the handicapping committees of her day as 'Black Diamond' the Yachting World hard-chine day-boat, and much later on the Stephen Jones designed Prism 28 'Thrust' which in the 1990's was to break all previous records for the trip to Ostend.

The 15 year old 'St George' was so heavily handicapped, David recalls, that her rating was higher than the maximum allowed for a One Tonner.

'St George' came into David's possession for the vast sum of £300, after lying neglected in Petticrows yard at Burnham. He remembers being eternally grateful to Harry Pye of the RBYC and something of a father figure to young sailors, who stepped in and managed to beat down the price by £100 by offering to write out a cheque on the spot.

'St George' was followed by Stella No. 33 'Astra' in which David won the Round the Goodwins Race in 1966.

Later boats included the 28ft 'Sjohast' - " a lovely boat, no engine. I had two of them, the second was not as successful..."

After more than 20 years of EAORA racing he made the first of many subsequent appearances amongst the season's trophy winners in 1987 with the X102 'Fiona of Burnham' in which he won the Barnard Cup for Class II and the overall season's championship in 1987 and 1988. And so it went on.

Although he was not to win the overall championship again for almost ten years (1997 with the J35 'Fiona' VII) David was unbeatable in Class II from this time on, taking the Barnard Trophy five further years in succession.

The eighth and current 'Fiona' is a Prima 38 which rates in Class I and David's winning streak continued amongst the larger opposition to give him a grand total of thirteen class trophies in eleven years and five overall championships.

In addition to carrying out almost a full programme of RORC racing on the South Coast each year David still continues to do enough East Anglian races to qualify, although he now races for the Royal Thames YC.

"It's the eccentric people that the sport attracts that make it so amusing" he says. Another notable competitor from the Royal Burnham is the ebullient Kit Hobday, with a succession of 'Bear's from the Stephen Jones three-quarter tonner 'Erotic Bear' and the GK34 'Geriatric Bear' to the Sigma 400 and later the

Doing it in style! Kit Hobday; Tim Louis and Mike Patten at the launch of 'Independent Bear'

'Fiona VII' Cowes Week 1992

Corby 41 'Independent Bear' which he co-owns with Tim Louis.

Kit started his sailing life at Thorpe Bay where he returned from Army service to revive the club's fortunes, oversaw the building of a new clubhouse and became Commodore at the early age of 40.

Always a tough competitor he was twice a winner and three times a runner-up of the Hornet world champion, and was involved in four successful defences of the C Class Catamaran America's Cup, before moving into the Soling class, and later into offshore racing.

He later became deputy chairman for two British attempts at the America's Cup, firstly with 'Lionheart' and later with Peter De Savary and 'Victory of Burnham' all of which fall well outside the scope of an East Anglian history.

The latest 'Bear' a Farr 52 to be known as 'Bear of Britain' was launched in April 2001, by the Duke of York in his capacity as Commodore of The Royal Thames YC

It is hoped that her principal mission will be to encourage young talent and newcomers to the sport in a new international and non-professional "Admiral's Cup-type" match racing competition sponsored by The Royal Thames.

Another family from the early days still making waves in the East Anglian scene into the Eighties were the Herrings from Royal Burnham, who gave their name to the club's Ralph Herring Trophy.

The trophy was won for the first time in 1951 by Phil Herring sailing 'Lora' while brother Ralph was second with 'Andante'.

After 'Lora' the family purchased 'Whiplash' a North Sea 24 originally designed by Kim Holman and built in Burnham by Tucker Brown. 'Whiplash' was a consistent performer on the EAORA circuit for many years in the hands of Phil and his son

'Bear of Britain' - *Photo courtesy of Hugh Bourn*

'Crusader'- The converted 12 metre

Tim and daughter-in-law Cathy.

In the early Eighties the family moved up a gear, with the chartered One Tonner 'Ark'. Then, in a supreme effort to win a place in the 1985 British Admiral's Cup team Tim and Cathy followed 'Ark' with a one-off designed by Julian Everitt. 'Backlash' was launched at Cowes with typical panache at a memorable day-long party. By any standards it was a remarkable campaign for any family, undertaken to mark Tim and Cathy's Silver Wedding.

Although they did not achieve the main objective of making the British team, the family enjoyed an epic year during which 'Backlash' made two Transatlantic crossings (to take part in the SORC series) and sailed more than 16,000 miles.

Some of these miles were sailed in East Anglian waters, where 'Backlash' took the coveted Town Cup in Burnham Week in three successive years thus improving on the record set by his uncle Ralph and father Phil (EAORA chairman 1958/9) with 'Minstrel Maid'. The fall-out from British efforts to mount a successful America's Cup campaign had repercussions for the East

Coast in 1991 when Richard Matthews of West Mersea acquired Graham Walker's unsuccessful challenger the 12 Metre 'White Crusader' and announced his intention of converting her, and racing on the EAORA circuit, despite the drawbacks imposed by a keel drawing some 12ft.

Despite the misgivings 'Crusader' proved a great success in her new guise as an offshore racing yacht, winning the overall championship in 1991, and setting

Changing shapes in yacht design - 'Odd Job'

'Thrust' 1999

some remarkable times in the process. Indeed in an interview in 'Yachts & Yachting' in 1997 Richard declared that he had had as much, if not more fun with 'Crusader' than with any other boat he had owned. 'Crusader' completed at least three Fastnet races, and made EAORA history when she completed the crossing from Harwich to Ostend in a mind-boggling 8 hours 13 minutes and 35 seconds!

Nevertheless, keen to experiment with the latest technology Richard returned in 1997 to Stephen Jones for a new light displacement boat 'Essex Girl' which would do well in light airs.

There was also plenty of competition in the smaller end of the fleet. The most potent of these was 'Oddjob' an early Stephen Jones quarter-tonner bought by Nigel Theadom, a professional rigger, from Haven Ports YC which won the Class III 1990 and 1991. 'Odd Job' was followed with equal success in 1994 by 'Djinn Seng' and in 1996 by the SJ320 'Crikey!' the first of a succession of boats bearing an ever longer trail of exclamation marks. The 1991 season also saw a resurgence of interest in three-quarter tonners from South of the Thames with Peter Jackson's 'Oblivion Express'; Peter Pearson's 'Smokehaze' and the veteran SJ35 'Intention' campaigned by the Galloper Syndicate, all from the Royal Temple.

Slightly later from the same club came David Elderfield's innovative 'Baby Train' with her lifting keel, which was followed by 'Wavetrain'.

But it was designer Stephen Jones' new breed of lightweight flyers which really made East Coast sailors sit up and take notice.

Although theoretically equipped with accommodation and classed as cruiser/racers, these newcomers in practice sealed the fate of conventional offshore racing.

It was only a short step to the Sportsboat. The pace was set with the Prism 28 'Thrust' for Malcolm Struth of West Mersea.

Malcolm, a longstanding competitor with his father in 'Silver Shadow' which took Class II honours in1978, had been out of the racing scene for a few years, but now with a family of tough young sons he was ready for something ground-breaking.

'Thrust' in her bright yellow livery, with a huge draft,

Dave Hunkins winning team from 'Morning All' - winners of the Buckley Goblets

massive rig and low freeboard, and looking barely large enough to contain the crew, was certainly that.

'Thrust' put even the 65ft 'Crusader's' time to Ostend into perspective, with a record run of 11 hours 38 minutes to Ostend in the 1993 Buckley Goblets.

The following year, when the same race offered a full north-westerly gale 'Thrust' took just 8 hours 6 minutes and 27 seconds to cover the 95 miles from West Mersea, on her way to the overall season's championship.

'Thrust' was followed by the Prism 26 'Jiminy Cricket' an even smaller competitor from the same stable, sailed by Mike and Barbara Harrison and their growing sons from the Crouch YC.

Another potent performer was sail-maker Matthew Vincent's Castro designed 'Miss Piggy'. In Class I designer Andrew Stewart was experimenting with modifications to the earlier Lightwave 395 design for his brother Robbie.

The optimised result was 'Blush' which came into her own in 1993 taking both the Overall and Class I championship, after 12 races in a needle season against the veteran S & S34 'Morning All' which was not settled until the last race.

From the same drawing board in 1998 came 'The Geek' another innovative design in the race to find the fastest, lightest hull shape.

Old-timers simply could not believe their eyes when this 'little old dinghy' as Robbie always described 'The Geek' turned out to race in Class I, and came storming home to take the overall championship in 1998.

The huge disparity in performance (and particularly accommodation) between these new designs and the more traditional cruiser/racer almost inevitably gave rise to tensions, and an ever widening gap between those who wanted more suitable racing for these new designs, and those who still favoured the old ways.

This, combined with the economic and social pressures of the period, soon led to increasing calls for a more structured season, with shorter races which could be completed in one day from the same port, and did not involve delivery trips up and down the coast.

The first taste of things to come hit the Association in 1993, when Chris Goldsmith of Haven Ports announced new plans for the club's Cork Sand Race, normally run as a back to back weekend with the Walton & Frinton YC's Walton Trophy.

Both clubs, he said, now wished to re-cast the event as an Open Weekend, which they hoped would attract additional entries from boats which normally turned out for the successful Haven Series.

The Walton Trophy would be sailed as a normal race, but the Cork Sand would be run as two inshore round the cans events, with results amalgamated to count as one qualifying race for EAORA.

The backbone of East Anglian sailing. Left to right:
Mike Spear; David Edwards; David Powell; Nick Greville and Roy Aspinall

Despite some concerns about this being allowed to count, and worries about non-EAORA boats creating an obstruction on the line, the committee voted to give the project the go-ahead by 8 votes to 2.

Although the Harwich weekend turned out to be a great success, it was by no means universally accepted as an integral part of the season.

A stormy annual meeting failed to agree on anything, but it was clear that despite a spirited rearguard action by owners who were desperate to retain the long offshore element, the majority favoured some sort of change.

The chief of these should be to make races as interesting as possible, regardless of length, with plenty of corners and cross-tide legs.

Three long serving East Anglian Secretaries. Left to right: Jill Hill; Joan McKee and the author Jan Wise

The new committee's ambitions were bolstered by the results of a questionnaire compiled by Chris Goldsmith, the incoming chairman, which was circulated amongst both owners and crews.

Discussions at the 1994 annual general meeting centred on proposals to split the programme with a long and a short series of races, each with their own trophies. The overall championship would be decided by combining the points.

A draft programme was agreed which provided for 15 races, nine to count for the overall trophy, and two series of eight races each, of which six would count. One race could be counted for either series.

It was hoped that the Long Series would satisfy the

demands of the hard core of traditionalists, especially as it included the North Sea Race (in this case the 50th anniversary race). Meanwhile supporters of the short series set about considering venues for a second 'Haven Weekend'.

Nobody could have tried harder to meet the disparate needs and desires of all competitors, but by the end of 1995 it was clear the new arrangements had raised almost as many problems as they solved.

Dividing the season into A and B series, with a requirement for results from both series to win the overall championship, simply meant that keen owners found themselves committed to doing both series.

Fifteen races spread over ten weekends from May to early September was much too onerous a programme, particularly when owners were also keen to have a crack at Cowes, Ramsgate or the new and increasingly attractive biennial Cork Week. But there was no doubt that the new arrangements did encourage more owners to come out to play. On a happier note, in 1995 the Royal Burnham put a Royal spin on their Centenary year when HRH Prince Philip, the Duke of Edinburgh fired the starting gun for the club's joint race with the RORC to Ostend.

More than 100 boats took part in the 1996 season, with the inshore series prompting a healthy increase of entries in Class III from boats which would never dream of doing a long offshore event. The overall champion was Ian Hart and the crew of the Contessa 33 'Ace of Hearts III' while the Inter-Club Trophy which still depended on good results in both series went to the Crouch Yacht Club for the first time since 1987.

Indeed the club could congratulate itself on having turned out 58 starters in inshore events and 36 in the offshore series, and in the next few years was to take the inter-club team trophy twice more.

Despite all this the rift between the two schools of thought continued to grow, and by the following season had led to a complete split, and the formation of a new organisation, known as Sail East, which was entirely dedicated to short inshore racing.

Divided into four weekends in different parts of the East Coast from Harwich to Ramsgate, Sail East provides eight days of round the cans racing which has clearly met a demand, and attracted a considerable following.

EAORA continued to stick to its guns, with a programme which includes most of the longest-established East Coast races, each sponsored as always by one of their member clubs.

By careful nurturing and a close attention to dove-tailing fixtures into a logical sequence to meet some of the pressures of twenty-first century life, the Association has managed to maintain a small but loyal core of competitors, and in their 51st season there remains every reason to expect the support to continue, and to grow.

What goes around, comes around, and the recent arrival of a number of new boats gives plenty of cause for optimism.

EAORA CHAIRMEN
1950 - 2001

1950 - 52	Martin Slater
1952 - 55	Donald Spear
1955 - 58	Alan Baker
1958 - 59	Phil Herring
1959 - 63	W. Noel Jordan
1963 - 66	Vernon Powell
1966 - 69	Mike Spear
1969 - 72	Jack Williams
1972 - 75	Guy Clarabut
1975 - 78	David Edwards
1978 - 81	Brian Foulger
1981 - 84	David Barham
1984 - 87	David Powell
1987 - 90	Patrick Lee
1990 - 93	Peter Clements
1993 - 96	Chris Goldsmith
1996 - 98	Roy Aspinall
1999 - 2001	Stephen Gosling

Honorary Secretaries:

1950 - 52	G.Brian Humby
1952 - 55	H.C.Thomas
1955 - 63	Alan Buchanan
1963 - 68	Mrs P. Buchanan
1968 - 73	Joan McKee
1973 - 82	Jill Hill
1982 - 94	Jan Wise
1994 - 96	Sheena Burney
1996 - 97	Julia Dyer
1997 - 98	Catherine Mattison
1998 - 00	Andrea Treat
2001 -	Jan Wise

EAORA TROPHY WINNERS
1950-2000

INTER-CLUB CHAMPIONSHIP

1950	West Mersea Yacht Club	1976	West Mersea Yacht Club
1951	West Mersea Yacht Club	1977	West Mersea Yacht Club
1952	Maylandsea Bay Yacht Club	1978	West Mersea Yacht Club
1953	West Mersea Yacht Club	1979	West Mersea Yacht Club
1954	Royal Corinthian Yacht Club	1980	West Mersea Yacht Club
1955	West Mersea Yacht Club	1981	West Mersea Yacht Club
1956	Royal Corinthian Yacht Club	1982	West Mersea Yacht Club
1957	West Mersea Yacht Club	1983	West Mersea Yacht Club
1958	West Mersea Yacht Club	1984	Royal Burnham Yacht Club
1959	Royal Naval Sailing Ass.	1985	West Mersea Yacht Club
1960	Royal Burnham Yacht Club	1986	Crouch Yacht Club
1961	Royal Burnham Yacht Club	1987	Crouch Yacht Club
1962	West Mersea Yacht Club	1988	Royal Burnham Yacht Club
1963	Royal Burnham Yacht Club	1989	Haven Ports Yacht Club
1964	West Mersea Yacht Club	1990	Royal Burnham Yacht Club
1965	Royal Burnham Yacht Club	1991	Royal Burnham Yacht Club
1966	Royal Burnham Yacht Club	1992	West Mersea Yacht Club
1967	Crouch Yacht Club	1993	Royal Burnham Yacht Club
1968	West Mersea Yacht Club	1994	Haven Ports Yacht Club
1969	West Mersea Yacht Club	1995	Haven Ports Yacht Club
1970	Crouch Yacht Club	1996	Crouch Yacht Club
1971	West Mersea Yacht Club	1997	West Mersea Yacht Club
1972	West Mersea Yacht Club	1998	Royal Burnham Yacht Club
1973	West Mersea Yacht Club	1999	Crouch Yacht Club
1974	West Mersea Yacht Club	2000	Crouch Yacht Club
1975	West Mersea Yacht Club		

E.A.O.R.A. CHAMPIONSHIP
BLACKWATER TROPHY
1950 - 2000

1950	Brambling	A.D.Spear & C.H.Thomas
1951	Naiande	V.Powell
1952	Brambling	A. D.Spear & C.H.Thomas
1953	Naiande	V.Powell
1954	Martha McGilda	W.N.Jordan
1955	Brambling	A.D.Spear & C.H.Thomas
1956	Martha McGilda	W.N.Jordan
1957	Taeping	A.H.& P.M.Buchanan
1958	Vashti	J.M.Laing
1959	Amoret	Lt.Cdr J.M.Lawson,RN
1960	Starlight of Mersea	R.G.Hill
1961	Lora	D.Edwards, D.M.Cuthbert & L.Bromley
1962	Vae Victus	K.Trent
1963	Vae Victus	K.Trent
1964	Twister of Mersea	C.R.Holman
1965	Bandit of Mersea	D.M.Powell
1966	Clarion of Wight	Sir Maurice Laing
1967	Cheetah	H.Croker
1968	Cheetah	H.Croker
1969	Morning After	R.G.Hill
1970	Golden Dragon	G.A.Blake
	Mersea Oyster	D.M.Powell
1971	Ricochet	J.Harrison
1972	Nenno	L.Crawley
1973	U.F.O.	R.Matthews
1974	Runaway Robber	M.Richardson
1975	Hylas	D.Edwards
1976	Mumbo Jumbo	R.Wigley
1977	Tumblehome II	A.Smith
1978	Tumblehome II	A.Smith
1979	Tramp	F.Reed
1980	Bright Spark	T.Swann
1981	Nadia	R.Matthews
1982	Oystercatcher	R.Matthews
1983	Oystercatcher	R.Matthews
1984	Oystercatcher	R.Matthews
1985	Clarionet	J.Breakell
1986	Clarionet	J.Breakell
1987	Fiona of Burnham	D.L.Geaves
1988	Fiona of Burnham	D.L.Geaves
1989	Born Free	J.Breakell
1990	Born Free	J.Breakell
1991	Crusader	R.Matthews
1992	Sorcery	R.Wigley
1993	Blush	R.&P.Stewart
1994	Thrust	M.Struth
1995	Miss Piggy	M.Vincent
1996	Ace of Hearts	I.W.Hart
1997	Fiona VII	D.L.Geaves
1998	The Geek	R.&P.Stewart
1999	Fiona VIII	D.L.Geaves
2000	Fiona VIII	D.L.Geaves

CLASS I
CARMEN CUP
1958 - 2000

1958	Mindy	N.D.Davis
1959	Sea Feather	H.M.S.Ganges
1960	Firecrest	L.T.Daniels
1961	Taitsing	A.H. & P.M.Buchanan
1962	Vae Victus	K.Trent
1963	Vae Victus	K.Trent
1964	Taitsing	A.H.&P.M.Buchanan
1965	Othona	J.C.Stanley
1966	Clarion of Eight	Sir Maurice Laing
1967	Vendetta	D.Clarabut
1968	Cervantes III	R.C.Watson
1969	Xuxu	D.C.Barham
1970	Mersea Oyster	D.M.Powell
1971	Matambu	L.D.Brook
1972	Nenno	L.Crawley
1973	Formosa	W.H.Hawkins
1974	Morningtown	R.G.Hill
1975	Hylas	D.Edwards
1976	Mukluks	R.Dreschfield
1977	Mischief of Mersea	A.Hills
1978	Mischief of Mersea	A.Hills
1979	Oystercatcher 79	R.Matthews
1980	The Red Dragon	J.Wiltshier
1981	Nadia	R.Matthews
1982	Oystercatcher	R.Matthews
1983	Carronade	P.Clements
1984	Sidewinder	J.C.Oswald
1985	The Red Dragon	P.F.Lee
1986	Sidewinder	J.C.Oswald
1987	The Red Dragon	P.F.Lee
1988	The Red Dragon	P.F.Lee
1989	Sorcery	R.Wigley
1990	Born Free	J.Breakell
1991	Warlord	P.Tolhurst & C.Goldsmith
1992	Sorcery	R.Wigley
1993	Blush	R.&P.Stewart
1994	Fiona VII	D.L.Geaves
1995	Fiona VII	D.L.Geaves
1996	Fiona VII	D.L.Geaves
1997	Fiona VII	D.L.Geaves
1998	The Geek	R.&P.Stewart
1999	Fiona VIII	D.L.Geaves
2000	Fiona VIII	D.L.Geaves

CLASS II
BARNARD CUP
1953 - 2000

1953	Watertrekker	L.G.Polturak
1954	Martha McGilda	W..N.Jordan
1955	Taeping	A.H.&P.M.Buchanan
1956	Martha McGilda	W.N.Jordan
1957	Taeping	A.H. & P.M.Buchanan
1958	Vashti	J.M.Laing
1959	Vashti	J.M.Laing
1960	Vashti	J.M.Laing
1961	Lora	D.Edwards, D.M.Cuthbert & L.Bromley
1962	Viking of Mersea	R.G.Hill
1963	Cyprinus	R.G.Hill
1964	Maleni	M.D.Spear
1965	Andorran	D.Edwards & Lord Chelmer
1966	Dauber	R.J.H.Stewart
1967	La Bamba	H.Woods
1968	Whisperer	H.Woods
1969	Morning Cloud	Edward Heath
1970	Mornington	R.G.Hill
1971	Midas of Mersea	R & B Pearson
1972	Sootica	J.A.Sampson
1973	Carronade	P.&E.Clements
1974	U.F.O.	R.Matthews
1975	Whiplash	P.&T.Herring
1976	Contentious Spirit	P.Evans
1977	Tumblehome II	A.Smith
1978	Silver Shadow II	R.W.Struth
1979	Carronade	P.&E.Clements
1980	Bright Spark	T.Swann
1981	Senta of Mersea	A.Antcliff & G.Rankin
1982	Bright Spark	D.M.Powell
1983	Oystercatcher	R.Matthews
1984	Oystercatcher	R.Matthews
1985	Silver Spirit	R.W.& M.Struth
1986	Clarionet	J.Breakell
1987	Fiona of Burnham	D.L.Geaves
1988	Fiona of Burnham	D.L.Geaves
1989	Fiona of Burnham	D.L.Geaves
1990	Fiona of Burnham	D.L.Geaves
1991	Fiona of Burnham	D.L.Geaves
1992	Fiona of Burnham	D.L.Geaves
1993	Fiona of Burnham	D.L.Geaves
1994	Thrust	M.Struth
1995	Crikey	N.Theadom
1996	Crikey	N.Theadom
1997	Sir Jasper	S.&A.Weekes
1998	Shoot the Bar	C.J.Mills
1999	Shoot the Bar	C.J.Mills
2000	Shoot the Bar	C.J.Mills

CLASS III
GUNFLEET CUP
1958 - 2000

1958	Amoret	Lt. Cdr. J.A.Lawson,RN
1959	Amoret	Lt Cdr. J.A.Lawson, RN
1960	Starlight of Mersea	R.G.Hill
1961	Starshell	J.A.Sampson
1962	Starshell	J.A.Sampson
1963	Nymphet	L.D.Brook
1964	Twister of Mersea	C.R.Holman
1965	Bandit of Mersea	L.D.Brook
1966	Brigand Chief	D.Cole
1967	Cheetah	H.Croker
1968	Gunsmoke	J.Harrison
1969	Williwaw	R.G.Pitcher
1970	Huckleberry	J.Blackall
1971	Richochet	J.Harrison
1972	U.F.O.	R.Matthews
1973	U.F.O.	R.Matthews
1974	Runaway Robber	M.Richardson
1975	D'Arcy Spice	J.M.Pugh & Baker
1976	Mumbo Jumbo	R.Wigley
1977	Nimfo	D.Pye & M.Fellows
1978	Tumblehome II	A.Smith
1979	Nenno	L.Crawley
1980	Santa Evita	P.F.Lee & T.Vernon
1981	Wizard	R.Wigley
1982	Hesitation Roll	L.Jones
1983	Harmony	M.Holmes & T.Allen
1984	Harmony	M.Holmes & T.Allen
1985	Bright Spark	D.M.Powell
1986	Harmony	P. J.Dyer
1987	Local Hero II	R.J.Beales
1988	Secrets	R.A.Stewart
1989	Smiffy	D.N.Stearn
1990	Odd Job	N.Theadom
1991	Odd Job	N.Theadom
1992	Scarlet of Arun	N.& S.Holland Brown
1993	Morning All	D.Hunkin
1994	Djinn Seng	N.Theadom
1995	Miss Piggy	M.Vincent
1996	Ace of Hearts III	I.W.Hart
1997	Rainbow	D.Ellis
1998	Ace of Hearts III	I.W.Hart
1999	Ace of Hearts III	I.W.Hart
2000	Beatnik	E.Orris

CLASS IV
GOZZETT CUP
1977 - 1988

1977	Rampant Robber	A.&S.Jardine
1978	Hot Shot	C.&A.Brooke
1979	Rampant Robber	S.Jardine
1980	Espada	M.Evers
1981	Magical Mr M	T.Vernon
1982	Silent Movie	P.Worthington
1983	Magical Mr M	C.C.Simmonds
1984	Magical Mr M	C.C.Simmonds
1985	Magical Mr M	C.C.Simmonds
1986	Supernova	D.W.Jones
1987	Eclipse	D.&S.Cowan
1988	Sensor	D.Chatterton

BETA DIVISION
LIBYA CUP
1969 - 2000

1969	Stardust	R.Chadney
1970	Maleni	M.D.Spear
1971	Dione	J.Avery
1972	Matambu	L.D.Brook
1972	Shaker	J.Gozzett
1973	Oliva	K.Layzell
1974	Mar del Norte	R.S.Aspinall
1975	Whiplash	P.&T.S.Herring
1976	Whiplash	P.&T.S.Herring
1977	Nenno	L.Crawley
1978	Periwinkle	G.Chapman
1979	Richochet	J.Clifton
1980	Whiplash	P.&T.S.Herring
1981	Voile D'Or	A.J.Major
1982	Sunstone	T.&V.Jackson
1983	D'Arcy Spice	J.M.Pugh
1984	Scamper	R.Macnamara
1985	Clarionet	J.Breakell
1986	Voile D'Or	A.J.Major
1989	Fiona of Burnham	D.L.Geaves
1990	Fiona of Burnham	D.L.Geaves
1994	Djinn Seng	N.Theadom
1995	Moustique	M.D.Spear & A.J.Major
1996	Prairie Oyster	J.Mattison
1997	Scarlet Jester	S.Gosling
1998	Prairie Oyster	J.Mattison
1999	Gironde	P.Wood
2000	Sensor	D.Chatterton & J.Warren

EAST ANGLIAN WEEK
COUNTY STANDARD TROPHY
1981 - 2000

1981	Senta of Mersea	A.Antcliff & G.Rankin
1982	Geriatric Bear	C.C.Hobday
1984	Erotic Bear	C.C.Hobday
1986	Carronade VI	P.Clements
1987	Jiminy Cricket	M.Harrison
1988	Intention	Galloper Syndicate
1989	Sidewinder	J.C.&M.Oswald
1990	Sensor	Mr&Mrs D.Chatterton
1991	Carronade	P.Clements & H.Spero
1992	Sensor	Mr&Mrs D.Chatterton
1993	Independent Bear	C.C.Hobday
1994	Djinn Seng	N.Theadom
1995	Crikey	N.Theadom
1996	Sir Jasper	S.&A.Weekes
1997	Sensor	Mr & Mrs D.Chatterton
1999	Crikey!	N.Theadom
2000	Sensor	D.Chatterton & J.Warren

WINNERS OF THE STAR TROPHY

This cup, previously known as the Crouch YC Maximum Points Trophy was converted in 1973 into an annual award for meritorious acts of seamanship or consistent but unrewarded performance.

1974 - Bill Chapman, 'Flamingo'
1975 - Roger Chadney, RHYC, 'Stella Stardust'
1976 - Charles Chapman, RBYC, 'Autumn Breeze'
1977 - 1979 - Not awarded
1980 - Richard Oxley, Crouch YC, 'Red Shamrock'
1981 - John & Bridget Watkinson, RCYC, 'Golden Silence'
1982 - Not awarded
1983 - Len Baker, RBYC, 'Fine Fettle'
1984 - T.J.Green, HPYC, 'Hud'
1985 - John & Bridget Watkinson, RCYC 'Golden Silence'
1986 - Mike Chamberlain, MYC, 'Tom Bombadil'
1987 - Roy Aspinall, WMYC, 'Bellerophon of Mersea'
1988 - James Mattison, RBYC, 'Prairie Oyster'
1989 - P.Jackson & P.Woolnough, MLSC 'Grace & Danger'
1990 - Doug Ellis, HPYC, 'Rainbow'
1991 - Jonathan Leggett, HPYC, 'Chimp'
1992 - Roger Utting and Rudi Polednik, HPYC, 'Brandy Bottle'
1993 - Stephen Gosling, RBYC, 'Scarlet'
1994 - Frank Reed, WMYC, 'Tramp'
1995 - Paul Trudgett & John Brooking, HPYC, 'Space'
1996 - not awarded
1997 - Doug Ellis, HPYC, 'Rainbow'
1998 - not awarded
1999 - Phil Mounsey, CYC, 'Stella Peacock'
2000 - John Warren, WMYC, 'Putana'

ACKNOWLEDGMENTS

SOURCE MATERIAL

The Royal Ocean Racing Club: The First 75 Years
Ian Dear RORC *2000*
The History of the Royal Engineer Yacht Club
Maj.Gen. Sir Gerald Duke, *1982*
The Royal Harwich. A Short History of the RHYC
Frank Hussey, Boydell Press *1972*
A History of the Royal Burnham Yacht Club:
To mark the Jubilee of the Royal Title
RBYC *1988*
The West Mersea Yacht Club. A Centennial Chronicle
Dr N.R.Greville, WMYC *1999*
West Mersea Yacht Club 'Moliette' Newsletter
The Story of the Blackwater Sailing Club: The First Hundred Years
Jan Wise, BSC *1999*
Sailing. A Course of My Life
The Rt. Hon. Edward Heath, Sidgwick & Jackson *1975*
Three Boys in a Boat
David Brook, Adlard Coles *1968*
To Sea in Carpet Slippers
A.C.Sandison, Adlard Coles *1966*
Blackwater Men
Arthur & Michael Emmett, Seax Books *1992*
Fastnet Force 10
John Rousmaniere, WWNorton *1980*
Seahorse Magazine RORC *Dec. 1971*
Yachting World Annual *1960*
Yachts & Yachting *1983 - 2001*
Prime Clean Burnham Week Programme *1999*
Minute Books of the East Anglian Yacht Clubs Conference *1950-71*
Books of EAORA *1950 -94*